GREAT AUSSIE YARNS

WARREN FAHEY
& PETER LALOR

HarperCollins*Publishers*

HarperCollins*Publishers*

Great Aussie Yarns was originally published by HarperCollins as two separate books:
Classic Bush Yarns in 2001, and *Australian Beer Yarns* in 2002

This combined edition first published in Australia in 2006
by HarperCollins*Publishers* Australia Pty Limited
ABN 36 009 913 517
www.harpercollins.com.au

Classic Bush Yarns copyright © Bodgie Productions Pty Ltd 2001
The right of Warren Fahey to be identified as the author of this work has been
asserted by him under the *Copyright Amendment (Moral Rights) Act 2000.*

Australian Beer Yarns collection and arrangement copyright © Peter Lalor 2002
Copyright and moral rights in individual stories remain with the contributors
Cartoons by Warren Brown

HarperCollins*Publishers*
25 Ryde Road, Pymble, Sydney, NSW 2073, Australia
31 View Road, Glenfield, Auckland 10, New Zealand

National Library of Australia Cataloguing-in-Publication data:

Fahey, Warren.
Great aussie yarns.
  ISBN 13: 978 0 7322 8509 8.
  ISBN 10: 0 7322 8509 7.
  1. Short stories, Australian. 2. Australian poetry.
  3. Australian wit and humor. I. Lalor, Peter, 1963– . II. Title.
A820.8

Cover image of dog ha00048 © Gettyimages; all other images © Shutterstock
Cover design by Darren Holt, HarperCollins Design Studio
Printed and bound in China by Everbest on 80gsm Woodfree

6 5 4 3 2 1   06 07 08 09

CONTENTS

BUSH
YARNS

ABOUT WARREN FAHEY

Warren Fahey claims to be a graduate from the School of Hard Knocks and the Dingo University. He is also well known as a folklorist, author, broadcaster and performer of bush songs.

Warren is still collecting Australian yarns and would welcome
contributions for future publications.
To contact Warren Fahey and the Australian Folklore Unit:
www.warrenfahey.com

CONTENTS

ACKNOWLEDGMENTS

I am indebted to the many people who have allowed me to record their yarns. In particular, I thank Dick Roughley, Harold Anderson, Arthur Dalley, Rad Dawson, Joe Watson, Dave Matthias, Bart Saggers, Owen Judd, Frank Laurie, Bill Casey, Mossy Phillips, Graham Seal, Harry Stein, Bob Taylor of Rockhampton (for 'The Drinker's Dream'), Herb Green of St Lucia (for 'The Blackboy's Waltzing Matilda') and, of course, that greatest yarn spinner of all time, Anon. I would also like to salute the pioneering work of Bill Wannan, who started to collect and analyse the yarn tradition way back in the 1950s and whose books have always inspired and amused.

INTRODUCTION

The Australian sense of humour was born of convict blood, hopeful gold diggers, itinerant bush workers, canny swagmen, iron-backed bush women, laconic soldiers, sweaty factory workers and larrikin city slickers. Above all, it is the humour of a pioneering country where men, women and children battled with an idiosyncratic climate and the uncertainty of droughts, floods and bushfires was always present. It is a humour referred to as 'dry', despite much of it concerning the 'wet' of alcohol.

Our pioneers worked hard and played hard and believed in that old adage: if you can't laugh at yourself, then who can you laugh at?

The convicts had little to laugh about, yet they still found time to turn the horror in their lives into humour. The treadmills of Sydney must have been one of the cruelest devices of any penal system, yet our convicts laughingly referred to them as 'dancing academies'. Likewise, the cat-o'-nine-tails, a vicious whip that lacerated a man's back until the flesh was like quivering jelly, was known to the convicts as 'getting a new red shirt'.

The gold-rush days of the 1860s opened up Australia, and many a hopeful 'digger' believed you could simply 'pick up lumps of gold'. Eventually, they accepted the fact that 'there's gold out there alright, but there's a hell of a lot of earth mixed in with it'.

The itinerant bush workers carried their humour with them, making fun of station cooks, stingy station owners and whoever else stood in their way. The swag fraternity, always on the tramp and cadge, created a litany of humour turning hard times into howling times.

Although early Australian society was male-dominated, the feisty women of the outback were a mighty breed and had stories to match. Then there were our soldiers, who were highly regarded in war, yet neither Bluey nor Curley thought much about saluting or other such nonsense. As Australia grew, the population shifted from the bush to the cities, and the factory workers and city slickers also created a distinct sense of humour to add to the treasury.

This collection of stories is a sample of the Australian sense of humour and a good example of our living folklore. Although they are similar to jokes, and some have been circulated as such, they are quite different. These yarns are the descendants of a tradition of story-telling which has all but disappeared from modern life. They spin a tale, draw the listener in, and invite you to meet characters such as Lazy Len, Dad and Dave and Sandy the Shearer. They are the keys to our past and to our unique culture. Like all folklore, it evolves, which is why names, places and even endings change. Sometimes, yarns are localised to the teller's neighbourhood, and this also explains how real names and nicknames sometimes enter the picture.

Where do yarns come from? The same question can be asked of most folklore and the answer usually comes back to the average Tom, Dick or Harriet. We create and pass on folklore as an unconscious way of recording and documenting our travels as a society. Like songs, they have usually seen many 'owners' and experience a 'polishing' as they are passed on down through the years. Often the yarn-teller will inject his or her particular brand of humour into them; and at other times, they remain in their original form. Like jokes, they come and go with the times, only to be revived yet again when they are needed.

One could suspect that in this technologically obsessed age, we no longer need yarns. We have become a nation of people who 'get entertained', unlike in the old days when everyone had a 'party piece' they could perform. The majority of our entertainment now arrives neatly packaged via the electronic media — complete with predictable 'canned laughter'. Despite the dramatic social changes that have occurred in the last few decades, I believe humans desperately need stories in their lives. Story-telling and, in this case, yarn-telling, is something we can all participate in; it provides a unique opportunity for bridging the age barrier.

There is also the opportunity to impart traditional wisdom through such story-telling. One of the features of the yarn is that it tends to trick as the story unwinds. Yarns are not necessarily meant to be rib-tickling funny. They are more like vignettes of the funny side of life and, in this collection, the situations that formed the Australian identity, particularly in the nineteenth century when the bulk of our population lived in the country rather than the cities.

There is no escaping the fact that we live in an international world and that all cultures need to be protected. As an English-speaking country, we are continually under 'attack' from the cultural expressions of our neighbours — particularly America and Britain. We are exposed to an incredible flow of feature films, television programs, books, music and many other creations which affect the way we speak, what we say, how we see things and even what we wear. We are in the front line and there is no escaping, because we are already wearing our baseball hats back-to-front and telling others to 'Have a nice day'. We need to be continually reminded that we have our own history, our own way of speaking and our own way of identifying ourselves.

Like every country that produces folklore, it is through traditions and customs such as this that we can see who we are as a nation. Australians are unique and have an international reputation for being relaxed, casual and unpretentious. This is borne out in our yarns and the ways that we tell them. We should be thankful that, in so many ways, we are still a nation of bushwhackers.

It takes all types and we've got the bloody lot!

Warren Fahey
Folklorist

BUSH LOGIC

There is little doubt that Australia's unofficial national anthem is 'Waltzing Matilda'. A.B. 'Banjo' Paterson's story about the swagman who pinches a prime sheep for his campfire meal is known to every Australian worth his or her salt. It has a canny ability to stir up our nationalistic emotions like no other song. Who gives two hoots if it's about a sheep-stealing bush traveller who drowns himself in a billabong when he could simply have waded across to the other side and disappeared into the scrub!

The song is obviously written from the squatter's perspective, and real bush people know that in the swagman's *own* version he understandably turns on the squatter when accused of stealing one of the sheep.

'Listen mate, all I wuz doing was protecting myself from your savage sheep — I'd do the same again if another one of those bastards has a go at my ankles.'

In 1973, I was recording the songs and poems of Herb Green of St Lucia, Queensland, and he asked me if I'd ever heard the 'Blackboy's Waltzing Matilda'? I hadn't and it was a beauty.

THE BLACKBOY'S WALTZING MATILDA

Old fella bagman camp alonga billybung
Sitta longa shade big fella tree
Singum watchum old billy boiling
You'll come walkabout tildalonga me

You'll come a walkabout big fella roundabout
You come walkabout tildalonga me
Leadum dillybag meat froma tuckabag
You carry plurry swag tildalonga me

Up come a jimbuck to drink at the waterhole
Bagman tallem comalonga me
Singum shovim longa tuckabag
You come walkabout jumbuck longa me

Down come the troopie mounted on their prads
Down come a troopie one, two, three
Where's that jimbuck you got in your tuckabag
You come walkabout comalonga me

Bagman henup jumpa longa waterhole
Drown plurry self near big fella tree
Ghost him be seen all night be waterhole
You come walkabout tildalonga me.

There is a wonderful piece in Steele Rudd's *On Our Selection* in which the pioneering family are down on their luck and rations have been so depleted that they don't even have tea for the billy. Dad, ever the optimist, sits the family down and set about showing them how to make a special brew. He took a couple of slices of bread, toasted them pitch black, and proceeded to scrap the toast into the billy. After a few minutes, he sampled the brew and declared it to be 'quite tasty'.

The truth is, our pioneering families did survive the hardship of the outback by relying on sheer determination (and the occasional sack of flour from the neighbour) and the ability to battle through on next to nothing. Dad's tea probably tasted bloody awful, but not one of the Rudd family would have ever said so — that would have been tantamount to giving in.

Life in the bush was hell, as pioneers fought with drought, flood, bushfire, pestilence and the banks. Necessity definitely was the mother of invention and our survival bag-of-tricks included ingenious inventions, ranging from concertina-leggings to specially designed 'shoes' which enabled working dogs to cross the bindi-eye-infested grasslands. The bag-of-tricks also included a generous collection of folklore — yarns in particular. Pioneers used these yarns to bolster their confidence and to make them feel like they were not alone. A well-known character in a story helped them to share the frustration caused by having to roll up their sleeves and start again. It's like the old saying: if you can't laugh — then what hope is there?

Many yarns characterise bush dwellers as dull-witted and unsophisticated. This element of yarns is common to nearly all folklore, whether it be rural Americans from Hicksville, Chinese paddy-field toilers, Irish potato farmers or Britain's west-county workers. The odd thing is that in many of the yarns the joke is reversed, with the know-it-all city slicker coming off second best. Australian farmers have often been under-valued and we should always remember that supermarkets do not create bread, milk or any other staple in our diet. It is the farmer who feeds us all.

> *God bless the man who sows the wheat,*
> *Who finds its milk, fruit and meat,*
> *May his purse be heavy, his heart be light,*
> *His cattle, corn and ale go right,*
> *God bless the seeds his hands let fall:*
> *For the farmer he must feed them all.*
> (**Traditional song**)

GET OUT OF THE BLOODY RAIN!

The heavens had finally opened after many months of drought. One of the station hands yelped with excitement and rushed outside, where he jumped about with joy.

'Come in out of that rain, you bloody fool!' roared the station boss.

'But I'm not worried about getting wet, boss,' the young hand protested.

'I'm not worried about you,' the boss spluttered, 'but you're keeping the rain off the flamin' ground.'

PIPE WISDOM

Bert never took his treasured pipe out of his mouth. When he travelled down to Sydney, he was forced to share a rail carriage with a cranky old woman who objected to the pipe from the moment he sat down.

'I'll have you know that my husband is nearly seventy and never once has he put a pipe in his mouth.'

Bert thought about this as he gently sucked at the tobacco.

'That so, missus? I should tell you that I'm nearly eighty and I've never put it anywhere else.'

IT'S IN THE BIBLE

There were two chaps working down in Sydney. They knew each other from boyhood and they regularly arranged to have their holidays at the same time so they could go fishing on the south coast of New South Wales. One year, they decided to go west to the 'back country'. Eventually, they reached the township of Inari, which is about as outback as outback can be, and it was as dry as buggery — there wasn't a blade of grass to be seen and the paddocks seemed to be made of red dust. Fishing was obviously out of the question, so they made their way to the local pub to sink their sorrows in beer. Sitting on the verandah of the pub was a weathered old-timer who had a face as long as the Great Dividing Range.

'Good morning,' the lads offered.

The aged one just nodded in recognition.

'Pretty hot out here, isn't it,' they continued.

The old one looked at them and mumbled: 'A bit warm.'

'How the blazes do you live out here in this hell heat?'

'Do me,' the old one responded.

'Tell me,' enquired one of the city slickers, 'does it ever rain out here?'

The old boy took a long and disdainful look at the two of them, propped up his head and said: 'Did youse boys ever read in the Bible that bit where it rained for forty days and forty nights?'

'Yes, sir, we know that passage.'

'Well, Inari got fifteen points out of that bugger!'

THE FOX HAT

Prince Charles, the Prince of Whales and Dolphins, was to officially open the Jindywaroback Heritage Centre and there was lots of interest from the international press. When the time for the grand opening arrived, he came out on stage wearing a ridiculous-looking fox-fur hat — totally inappropriate for the Australian outback! Everyone attempted to be polite and not ask him about the hat until, at the civic reception, the local newspaper journalist couldn't hold back.

'Sir, I have one question and it is about your hat. Why are you wearing a fox-fur hat?'

Prince Charles looked sympathetically at the man and replied: 'I'm pleased you asked me that question because it has also puzzled me. Mummy told me to wear it. I was up very early to get the plane from Heathrow and as I left the castle, I knocked on Mummy's chamber door and told her I was off to Australia to open the Jindyworaback Heritage Centre, and I'm positive that she said: "Wear the fox hat!"'

SNAKE BITE

Bert and Bill were great mates going back some thirty years and they loved nothing better than to go bush for a week of fishing. They had planned a trip to a remote part of outback New South Wales where they had heard the codfish were monsters.

On the second day of their holiday, disaster struck. Bill had responded to the call of nature and while squatting behind a tree, he was bitten on the dick by a black snake which had, understandably, taken umbrage at being shat upon. Bill went into a panic as the snake slithered away, revealing its distinctive red belly.

'Bert! Bert! You've got to do something quick. Fetch a doctor!'

Bert could see that he would have to move fast, so he attempted to tie a tourniquet above the bite, and told Bill to try to rest while he went to get the Flying Doctor Service.

Off he raced towards the cattle station they had passed earlier, through the gates he tore, up the path to the homestead and asked to use the telephone.

The Flying Doctor Service is an admirable organisation, and contact was made immediately with the in-service doctor, who explained that although snake bites were commonplace, Bill would have to follow his instructions if he was to save his mate's life.

'Okay, okay, tell me what I have to do,' pleaded Bert.

The doctor told Bert that he must make a cut across the bite with a sharp knife and then suck the poison out of the wound. Bill would be okay if Bert followed these instructions.

Bill raced back to the campsite, down through the dusty tracks and down to the riverbank, where he found Bill in a desperate mood.

'What did he say? What do you have to do? What did the Flying Doctor say?' Bill screamed with obvious terror.

Bert looked at him, shook his head slowly, and said: 'Bill, he said you're going to die.'

ABORIGINAL CARVINGS

A tourist coach pulled up at Kakadu National Park and the coach driver informed the day-trippers about the beauty of the natural environment and how, further down the track, they could see some Aboriginal carvings. All the tourists scrambled out — except one old lady, who remained in the bus, concentrating on her knitting.

'Not coming, lady? Aren't you interested in seeing the Aboriginal carvings?' the driver enquired.

'No thank you, I've seen cow's calving — that was enough for me!'

A BIG FUTURE

The young station boy left school without learning to read and write and found himself down in the nearest town looking for work. After a week it became obvious that without these vital skills, he didn't have a lot of choice when it came to jobs, so he reluctantly applied for a position as a toilet attendant at the local factory. His duties were to wash down the toilets and keep a weekly record of all the cleaning products he used. After explaining that he couldn't write, the foreman told him he wasn't suitable for the job.

Dejected and rejected, he roamed the streets and finally sat down on an old wooden fruit case. As he pondered his frustrating situation, he became angry and kicked the fruit case to pieces. As he surveyed the damage, an idea struck him — to collect the pieces of wood and sell them as firewood. He made a few cents and decided to buy a few old crates from the local fruit shop. He chopped these up and sold them for firewood and made a few dollars. He continued buying and selling until he had enough money to go to the timberyard and buy some decent wood. Eventually, he had enough money to buy the timberyard.

As the years passed, he was able to buy the local forest and then he purchased timber holdings all over Australia. He had become a multimillionaire. The time had come for him to expand internationally, and while negotiating with America's largest mill operation, the company's head honcho insisted on a written agreement to seal the deal.

'Can't do that,' the Australian said. 'Never did learn to read or write.'

The American was dumbfounded. 'But you're the most successful timber merchant in Australia and a multimillionaire! For God's sake man, what would you have aspired to be if you had been able to read and write?'

The Australian looked long and hard at the American and replied: 'A toilet attendant.'

NEVER FELT BETTER

Drover Mike O'Hearn appeared in the Wee Waa District Court charged over his negligence in allowing his stock to stray all over the main road. A passing semitrailer had run right into the herd, killing several beasts and causing severe bodily injury to O'Hearn, his horse and his dog. Under cross-examination by the prosecutor, the drover confirmed that his first words to the attending police officer were: 'I've never felt better in my life.'

When asked to explain this strange comment, the drover said: 'Well, there I was, spread-eagled on the road, with a busted arm and leg and surrounded by this carnage. The police officer came up to my horse, which was bleeding from both nostrils and in great distress, put his pistol to its head and pulled the trigger. Then he went over to my dog, which was in an awful mess, and did the same. Then he walked over to me and said: "How are you, O'Hearn?" I took a look at his pistol and quickly responded: "I've never felt better in my life."'

SMART ALEC

The boss's son had been studying at a swank Sydney boarding school and was now back on the land. He'd been told to take Alec, an experienced jackaroo, out with him to check the boundary fences in the far paddocks. They had been riding for about three hours when the lad asked the jackaroo: 'Do you know anything about geology, Alec?'

'No, boss, don't know 'im at all.'

'Goodness, man, don't you coves know anything? A man might as well be dead.'

The jackaroo looked up and added: 'Yes, boss, might as well be dead.'

They had travelled for another couple of hours when the boss's son offered: 'Alec, do you know anything about biology?'

Alec looked up at the boss and said: 'Boss, don't know this biology, don't think he worked here by that name.'

'Good grief, man, without a knowledge of the sciences, a man might as well be dead.'

'Yes, boss, might as well be dead.'

Late in the afternoon, the heavens opened and the old creek became a swirling torrent. The jackaroo made his way to the water's edge, where he proceeded to undo his bridle reins and cross his stirrups over the pommel of his saddle. He then turned to the boss's son.

'Boss, you know anything about swimology?'

'No, I'm afraid not,' he replied.

'By cripes, boss, I think it's your turn to be bloody dead.'

LEAVING THE LAND

Bert, like many old stubborn bushies, took pride in the fact that he didn't give up easily but there he was, in the town pub, explaining why he was leaving the land for good.

'Yes, I've had the land and everything about the darned place. The first year wasn't so bad, except that the rabbits kept breeding so fast that they used the old anthills for burrows. The second year wasn't too good either, and the only way I kept afloat was by tying knots in the tails of all my cattle so they couldn't slip out through the fence. I even survived the third year, when I had to dig myself out of the red dust and it was such hard yakka that I wore me best shovel down to the size of a sugar scoop. I stuck through it all, thick and thin, but this last year was too bloody much for a man to bear. I knew my time was up when I spotted the grasshoppers arrive at my paddocks with their own packed lunches.'

HOLDING MY OWN

The bushies of yesteryear were extraordinary optimists, and this country was built on a pioneering spirit that never gave up. A farmer had tried to make his station pay its own way but he always seemed to be at odds with nature. In his first year he was hit by a severe drought, and in the second year the paddocks were washed away in a massive flood, which was followed a year later by a locust plague.

Despite all this devastation, the farmer kept up his spirits and started all over again. In the fourth year, a bushfire raged through the property and, yet again, he started over.

An old mate who he'd known for years came to visit. He looked around the station and finally asked: 'How're you doing?'

'Well,' drawled the farmer, 'I'm holding me own.'

The visitor looked around again and said: 'But how could you when there's no crop, no grass, and I haven't seen any stock. How could you be holding your own?'

'Well,' the farmer confided, 'I came here with bugger all and I've still got bugger all. I'm holding my own.'

A BLOWN VALVE

The station hand had bought a new wireless to keep his young family amused, and for three months he had trouble-free reception as they tuned into radio serials, quiz shows and the news of the world. Then one morning, the radio froze up and all he could get was static and garbled sounds. He took the wireless to town the next weekend and gave it to the radio repairman, who advised him that he could collect it the following Saturday. When the time came to collect the machine, he also received a bill for ten quid.

'What's this for?' he asked.

'A blown valve,' came the reply.

'Gosh, to think I have two kids and a wife at home and they still can't keep the blowflies out of the bloody thing!'

ONE-EYED PETE

Saltbush Pete was a renowned shearer and a determined drinker, and he'd signed on with a shearing crew way up bush. He had to catch the 5.00 a.m. mail train to get there, so he booked into the local Railway Hotel. Thinking a drink wouldn't hurt, he got stuck into the grog with a few mates. When he finally retired to catch a couple of hours sleep, his drinking mates thought they would play a trick on Pete, so they crept into his room and shaved off one of his bushy eyebrows. The publican shook him awake at 4.00 a.m. and Pete staggered to the washroom, where he gaped at his face and screamed: 'Oh Christ! They've woken the wrong bloody man!'

DE-DUCKS

The farmer had a look that would have soured milk when asked how his crops had turned out.

'De-ducks got the bloody crop.'

'Ducks!' the enquirer exclaimed in surprise.

'No,' was the reply, 'not ducks — de-ducks. I shipped a good number of truckloads of wheat all right, but the bastards de-ducks the road freight, they de-ducks the insurance, they de-ducks the handling charges, and when they gets through, I'm buggered if the de-ducks haven't got all of me money.'

COWS JUMP WHEN THEY WANT TO

A farmer had been out all night celebrating his local football team's victory over the neighbouring town's team. His hangover was fierce, however farm duties still had to be done. He rallied his aching body and staggered out to milk his cows. The herd, being a well-trained mob, were all waiting impatiently for their milking when the farmer staggered into the shed. He stood there swaying, holding his pounding head with both hands and trembling with the horrors.

His eyes and ears sprang open as a jersey cow stepped up to his side and said: 'You look terrible this morning.'

'You'd look bloody awful too if you'd had the night I've had,' the suffering farmer muttered.

'Well,' said the cow, 'you've always been quite decent to us ladies, so we'll do all we can to help you get through this. Just a minute.'

The cow had a hurried conversation with the herd, and then said: 'We're all agreed, all you have to do is take a firm grip, hang on tight, and we'll jump up and down. That should do it and then you can go back to bed.'

THE STRETCHED SNAKE

Kelly the bullocky was driving his dray along a rough bush track in outback New South Wales. He must have dozed off because, all of a sudden, he was aware that the wheels of the dray were passing over a large king brown snake. Nothing unusual in such an occurrence, so Kelly paid little attention and continued on his journey. On his return trip several days later, he happened to pass through the exact same spot, so he decided to try and find the snake's skin. He looked high and low but couldn't find a trace of the reptile and then, looking up, he smiled to himself and started to chuckle. He later told the story to his mates in the Nyngan pub.

'There it was, about six or seven feet above me, with its head wrapped around one tree and its tail around another. Somehow or other, it had managed to climb up the tree and swing its tail across to the other and then it stretched itself out and waited for its broken back to mend. It was a sight for sore eyes!'

His mates never quite believed him but they reckoned it wasn't an impossibility.

MOTH BALLS

An American tourist was visiting the outback and staying in a country pub. One day the hotel maid was cleaning his room when she opened the cupboard and a moth ball rolled out. This puzzled the Yank, who stared at the round white ball on the carpet.

'Say, missy, what is that white thing that rolled out of the cupboard?'

'That, sir,' replied the maid, 'is a moth ball.'

'Gee whiz,' said the surprised American tourist, 'some moth!'

BABBLING BROOKS

The old station cook slept when he wasn't working and worked when he wasn't sleeping.

They used to say that a station cook had to have three skills: an ability to get up early in the morning, a passing knowledge of cookery and, most importantly, a good pair of fighting fists. Not many people wanted the job of cooking for a team of grumbling, always hungry shearers, drovers or timber cutters. It was hard yakka with little reward. The shearers used to have a ballot system which they used to vote for the season's cook, and they paid him at the season's end. The job was usually reserved for the oldest and most useless man on the board, so it was rarely an honour.

Rations were often scarce and many an exasperated cook, waiting for the unreliable river boat that carried supplies, would resort to 'roo stew, wallaby stew and some stews too dubious to name here. The men were big eaters — consuming mountains of bread and gallons of hot, strong tea which they nicknamed 'Jack the painter' because of the dark brown stain it would leave around their mouths.

Breakfast was usually a big meal with lamb chops, bacon and eggs, lunch was another large hot meal, and in the evening was the inevitable stew followed by lashings of damper with jam or treacle and, if the supply boat had arrived, tinned peaches and condensed milk.

Of course, there were also some excellent cooks working in the outback. Many took immense pride in making impressive meals out of practically nothing. The cookhouse was always a flurry of activity with the fires in need of continual stoking, damper to be prepared and all that peeling, churning and slaughtering — because in most cases, the cook was also the butcher. Some cooks were characters who enjoyed a song and yarn-telling session or played a musical instrument, and others had reputations for irritable crankiness and extended silences. The Chinese were favoured as cooks, which might explain Australia's long-standing love affair with Chinese food.

There were also cooks who had worked in the big kitchens of the city hotels and found themselves in the bush — often with strict orders to 'dry out'. Surprisingly, alcohol was completely forbidden on nearly all outback stations. However, if anyone was to sneak some grog into the camp, it was usually the cook.

There are many stories about cooks going 'on a bender' and disappearing to the nearest hotel bar and staying there until they were collected. The publicans usually allowed these men to stay for a few days, then they would put the inebriated man into the 'dead house', which was usually a dark shed at the rear of the pub, where they sobered up and made themselves ready for the return to work.

THE COOK'S REVENGE

Once I took a job of cooking,
For some poddy-dodging cows,
But of all the little jobs I've had,
It took the cake for rows.

The bloody meat was gone bad,
And the cake it was a sod,
For the damper had gone ropy,
It was, so help me Bob.

The tea it looked like water,
And the pudding just as bad,
And every time we forked it on,
It made us fellows mad.

One day I thought: 'I'll square things!'
And let them see no mug was I,
So I mixed some sniftin' pea soup,
To make them fellows cry.

Half a tin of curry,
To give the stuff some grip,
And half a tin of pepper,
To make them fellows shit.

And half a tin of cow dung,
Singed to make it look like toast,
The stink of it would knock you down,
Like Jesus Holy Ghost!

So the stockmen came in early,
If no tucker — look out for us,
Just hop in here you stockmen boys,
For I'll bring some soup to light.

So the plate full each they took,
By cripes it tastes all right,
But nothing like the second helping
To make those bastards shite.

They shat upon the tables,
They shat upon the floor,
The dirty rotten bastards —
They never asked for more.

So I snatched my time,
And wandered down the line,
So if you're looking for a first class cook —
I'm waiting for a job!

THE CANE-CUTTERS' LAMENT

How we suffered grief and pain,
Up in Queensland cutting cane.
We sweated blood, we were black as sin,
And the ganger, he drove the spurs right in.

The first six weeks, so help me Christ,
We lived on cheese and half-boiled rice,
Doughy bread and cat's-meat stew,
And corn beef that the flies had blew.

The Chinese cook with his cross-eyed look,
Filled our guts with his corn-beef hashes.
Damned our souls with his half-baked rolls,
That'd poison snakes with their greasy ashes.

The cane was bad, the cutters were mad,
And the cook, he had shit on the liver.
And never again will I cut cane,
On the banks of the Queensland river.

WASN'T ME, SAID THE NEW COOK

The missus on Wallandamper Station was widely regarded as a tough operator. One morning, she comes bawling and whining into the men's quarters and obviously upset about something or other. She eyed the new cook with one of those looks that could kill.

'Who was it?' she demanded. 'Who left the soap to disintegrate in the dishwater? It was you, wasn't it, Cookie?'

All eyes turned to the new cook.

'Nar missus, t'wasn't me and I can prove it. I've only been here a week and I definitely have not washed me hands!'

GREASY SOL

Some shearer's cooks carried a fearful reputation for never washing. Greasy Sol, a well-known character from around the Riverina area, was one such man. Once, he arrived at a new shed at the beginning of the season and one of the shearers commented that he was wearing the very same clothes he had been wearing at the end of last season. They reckoned he hadn't had a wash in years, so they decided to make him take a bath. They crept up behind him and jumped him. Seven shearers and two rousies held him down and they started to peel off his filthy clothing when all of a sudden, they saw a peculiar hump on his upper back. They continued to peel off the clothing and to their utter surprise they found a schoolbag. It was that long since he had washed!

BLUE STEW

There was a cook known throughout the eastern states as 'Blue Stew' Lou. He earned his nickname in an incident that occurred several years ago. Apparently, Lou had been on a bender, and for weeks he kept serving up the same boring lamb and carrot stew. The men swore he never cleaned the bottom of the pot and that he just kept adding to it day after day, week after week.

One day, the shearers decided to take matters into their own hands. They got a Reckitt's Blue Bag — the one that was added to the laundry copper pot on washing day. They crept into the kitchen and popped the bag into the stew pot, confident that this would mean the end of the infernal stew. That evening, as they assembled for their meal, Lou came out carrying the pot.

He plonked it down on the mess table and shouted: 'Well, my fine fellows, I have a surprise for you tonight — my famous "blue stew".'

EXTREMELY LIGHT PASTRIES

We had a famous cook up on our station one year. He had been the pastry cook at the Australia Hotel in Sydney and they had sent him out 'bush' to dry out. He was a marvellous cook. The only problem was that we had to keep the windows of the mess hut shut all the time because his pastries were so light that they kept floating out the windows.

STEW AGAIN!

Times were tough and the old cookie had to make do with what he could muster up as tucker. One of the saving graces of many meals was the ample supply of Worcestershire sauce which disguised the near-rotten mutton. One day, the boss looked deep into the stew pot and took the cook aside.

'I notice that the stew is getting pretty black. How do you work out the right amount of sauce?'

'Oh, it's not too difficult. I gets the old billygoat and I ties him upwind at the rear of the cookhouse, and I then set the stew pot downwind and then I steps in the dead centre line. If I smell the goat before the stew, then I know she needs more sauce.'

BUSHIES DOWN IN THE BIG SMOKE

There is a whole genre of yarns about bush folk venturing to the city or, as it is generally known, the 'big smoke'. Bushies appear incapable of navigating their way around the city, or avoiding the temptation of gambling, sex and alcohol. They also seem to have difficulty finding their way back home with anything they had left with.

One classic tale concerns a family who travelled down to Sydney on the train, alighted at Central Station and proceeded straight to the legendary Grace Brothers department store. They stayed in the store for two weeks, sleeping in the bedding department, eating in the cafeteria, leaving the children in the toy department, and so on. Apparently, they had a marvellous time and told all their friends that Sydney wasn't that big after all!

There is no doubt that the city appeared overwhelming to many rural visitors, and most probably still is. If you lived on a station where the nearest neighbour was a hundred miles away, education for the kids was the crackling 'school of the air' on the radio, the closest one got to a department store was the occasional Afghan hawker, and the nearest hospital was the Flying Doctor Service, then a trip to the 'big smoke' was a definite shock to the system.

YELLOW PYJAMAS

The old bush prospector didn't come to town very often but when he did, he liked to spend time in the general store.

He was watching the shop owner unpack a delivery of stock when the old fellow spotted some bright yellow pyjamas.

'What's those things?' he enquired, looking at them curiously.

'These are pyjamas,' said the storekeeper.

'Yeah? What's they used for then?'

'For wearing at night. You wanna buy a pair?'

'Nah! No use to me, mate, I never goes out at night 'cept to bed.'

A NICE CAMPSITE

A young policeman walking through the Sydney Botanical Gardens spots two swaggies stretched out under some gum trees. They've got their washing drying on the nearby shrubs and they're just about to light a campfire.

'What the hell are you blokes doing? Where do you live?'

The first swaggie, a poetical fellow named Ponsombury, looks at the policeman and says: 'Everywhere.'

The policeman, clearly annoyed, stared at him and insistently asked: 'Where exactly do you live?'

'On the windblown mountains and sun-drenched plains, by the raging rivers and the open roads. Everywhere!'

'Alright, alright,' said the policeman. He turned his gaze to the other swaggie. 'What about you? Where do you live?'

'Me?' asked the second swaggie. 'I'm 'is next-door neighbour!'

OLD BILL IN THE BIG SMOKE

Old Bill was making his first trip to the big city and found himself in Myers. He was dazzled and he walked from floor to floor until he found himself in the women's clothing department. He stood there, totally mystified, staring as an elderly woman stepped into the changing rooms. A security guard approached him and asked him if anything was wrong, but Old Bill just gazed in amazement as a young girl emerged from the same changing rooms.

'Strike me pink! I'll be darned!' was all Old Bill could manage to say. 'I knew I should have brought the old lady with me.'

FORGET THOSE GRASSHOPPERS

The stockman had earned a spree in town and found himself in Sydney staying at the posh Australia Hotel. Not being able to read or write, he asked the waiter to bring him something nice to eat. The waiter, an obliging chap, returned with a large plate of Sydney Harbour prawns on a bed of shredded lettuce leaves. After awhile, the bushie signalled the waiter.

'Pierre, how much do I owe you for the tucker?'

'That will be one pound, sir.'

As the waiter handed the stockman his bill, he noticed that the prawns had all been pushed to one side of the plate, untouched.

'But sir, you didn't eat your meal, was there something wrong?'

'Well, the grass was just okay, but be blowed if I was going to eat the bloody grasshoppers!'

BIG 'UNS

One of those commercial traveller blokes had landed in Darwin, and a few of the hotel boarders decided to show him around their town.

'What d'yer think of our stockyards?' asked one.

'Oh, they're alright,' the salesman replied, 'but we have branding yards in New South Wales that are a lot bigger.'

Every time one of the locals pointed anything out the salesman would come back saying things were bigger and better down south.

That night they decided to teach him a lesson, so they put some tortoises in his bed.

When the traveller turned back his sheets, he exclaimed: 'What the hell are these?'

'Territorian bedbugs!' came the chorus.

The commercial traveller looked at the tortoises for a minute.

'So they are,' he agreed. 'Young 'uns, aren't they?'

THE BIG GUN SHEARER

The 'Big Gun' toiled with his heart and soul,
Shearing sheep to make a roll
Out in the backblocks, far away,
Then off to Sydney for a holiday.

Down in the city he's a terrible swell,
Takes a taxi to the Kent Hotel,
The barmaid says: 'You do look ill,
It must have been rough tucker, Bill.'

Down in the city, he looks a goat,
With his Oxford bags and his Seymour coat.
He spends his money like a fool, of course,
That he worked for like a bloomin' horse.

He shouts for everyone 'round the place,
And goes to Randwick for the big horse race.
He dopes himself on backache pills,
And talks high tallies and tucker bills.

And when it's spent he's sick and sore,
The barmaid's looks are kind no more.
His erstwhile friends don't give a hoot,
He goes back to the bush per what? Per boot!

Back in Bourke where the flies are bad,
He tells of the wonderful times he'd had.
He tells of the winners he shouldn't have missed,
And skites of the dozens of girls that he's kissed.

He stands on the corner cadging fags,
His shirt-tail showing through his Oxford bags.
He's pawned his beautiful Seymour coat,
He's got no money — oh, what a goat!

He's got no tucker and he can't get a booze,
The soles have gone from his snakeskin shoes.
He camps on the bend in the wind and the rain,
And waits for shearing to start again.

All you blokes with a cheque to spend,
Don't go to the city where you've got no friends.
Head for the nearest wayside shack,
It's not so far when you've got to walk back.

MICE PLAGUE

The shearer had earned a spree in town and headed down to Adelaide where he decided to hit the high spots. His first stop was a swish restaurant where he ordered tea and cake. The waitress delivered the tea and a lovely fresh caraway seed cake.

The shearer commented: 'I see you've had a mouse plague down here, too.'

HUNGRY TYSON IN PITT STREET

Hungry Tyson, the legendary wealthy grazier, was visiting Sydney when he accidentally dropped his wallet in Pitt Street. The police had to be called in to have it removed — it was blocking the traffic!

YOU WOULDN'T BELIEVE IT!

It happened a few years back — off the Newcastle, New South Wales, coastline. Five blokes decided to go fishing, out past the heads where they had been told they could catch 'the big 'uns'. The captain of the boat had given them a list of instructions, starting with the all-important fact that they should definitely have a solid breakfast — even if the boat was leaving at 3.30 a.m. Now that was all very well for a seasoned sailor to say, but you should try eating at some ungodly hour of the morning when your eyes insist on closing.

Off they sailed and about an hour later, they hit the swells and the fishing was terrific. An hour after that, there were even bigger swells. One of the blokes had obviously not eaten breakfast — he had broken the number one rule! There was all manner of retching and groaning as he threw up into the sea. Next thing, he turned to his mates and explained that as he had thrown up, his false teeth had accidentally tumbled into the briny. He looked a little like a gummy shark, and his mates couldn't help but laugh. This made the man even more miserable.

One of the men decided to play a prank on his friend, so he took out his own dentures and hooked them up to his fishing line and gently lowered them into the sea. Five minutes later, he shouted out that he had got a 'bite' and proceeded to wind up the line in full view of the sick feller.

'Whoa, what have I got here? God blimey, you wouldn't read about it! I think I've hooked your teeth!'

The sick one looked up, incredulous, and the colour was already coming back into his cheeks as he snatched the teeth and tried to place them in his mouth. All of a sudden, he chucks them overboard and comments: 'Wouldn't you know my luck — they're some other bastard's!'

THE FOOTY'S ON SUNDAY

The man was standing on the edge of Sydney's notorious suicide point, The Gap at Watson's Bay. Inspector Walty was experienced in talking would-be suiciders down from the cliff, and was trying to attract the man's attention.

'Don't do it. It's not worth it!' he yelled out.

'Go away!' responded the dejected man.

'Look, I know you're pained,' continued the policeman, 'but she's not worth it whoever she is.'

'It's not a woman,' came the agitated reply.

'Your job isn't worth your life,' yelled the policeman.

'Not my job,' responded the man.

This clearly isn't working, thought Walty as he scratched about for a different approach.

'Hey! What about the big match on the weekend. You wouldn't want to miss seeing the Swans play, would you?'

'Hate the Swans,' the reply bounced back.

'Jump you useless bastard, jump!' was the policeman's final offering.

UP IN THE AIR

Two of Australia's pioneer airmen, Charles Kingsford Smith and Bert Hinkler, spent considerable time travelling through outback Australia. Flying was a novelty back then, and the airmen would visit rural towns after flying over nearby farms and roadways inevitably startling cattle, horses and the population at large. Both famous airmen produced their own share of folklore, including some songs and poems.

When Hinkler flew his legendary Australia to Britain solo flight, he smashed all air records, prompting the following ditty.

> *Hinkle, Hinkle little star,*
> *Sixteen days and here you are!*

'SMITHY' FLIES IN

I remember when the great airman Charles Kingsford Smith visited Goondiwindi in the 1920s. It was his usual practice to circle the town to draw attention to his arrival. He used to charge ten shillings for a quick ride — a joy flight. Ten shillings was quite a lot of money in those days.

Anyway, 'Smithy' decided to take one of the local Aboriginal stockmen up for the first flight as a publicity stunt. When they were up there, he started to do acrobatics and funny stuff like flying upside-down. When they finally landed, there was a big crowd assembled and out steps Old Jimmy with his eyes popping out like organ-stops, and he was followed by Kingsford Smith.

They were both standing on the stage when Smithy turned to Jimmy and said: 'Well, Jimmy, I'm sure that was quite an experience for you. I bet that half the people down here thought that we were going to crash.'

Jimmy quickly turned to the crowd and announced: 'And, by cripes, Mr Kingsford Smith, half the people up there thought the bloody same!'

HUSTLING HINKLER

Two drovers were disturbed by the sound of Bert Hinkler's aeroplane as it buzzed the neighbouring township.

'Blasted silly things those aeroplanes. I'm damn certain you wouldn't catch me up there in one of those things!'

His mate kept gazing skyward, deep in thought, until he finally added: 'Well, you wouldn't catch me up there without one!'

FEATHERS

Hustling Hinkler was barnstorming outback South Australia and scaring the tripes out of the rural community. As he swooped over an outback property, the startled grazier leapt for his shotgun and immediately opened fire on the aeroplane as it dropped leaflets about the local air show.

Later that week, the grazier was in the pub recounting how he'd taken a shot at the flying bird.

'And did you get it?' one joker casually asked.

'Nah, but I got some of its feathers!'

REGULATIONS

The first commercial flight was set to take off from the new Atherton Tablelands Airport when a grumpy old stockman made his way down the aisle. He was lugging a well-worn saddle, a bridle and a large blanket roll.

'Sorry, sir,' the alarmed hostess apologised. 'You can't bring all that into the cabin.'

'That be darned,' the old boy grunted. 'You should be thankful I sold me bloody 'orse!'

THE FLYING DOCTOR

Old Bertie watched as the Flying Doctor flew over the property.

'When I was a young stockman, we didn't have any need for such fancy medicine and flying doctors. Once I was thrown from my horse and landed on a big tree, breaking about ten of my ribs. I was in a terrible state but the old Chinese cook fixed me up proper and good. He made me eat a couple of handfuls of rice and then drink two pints of bore water. The rice started to swell up in no time and eventually pushed my ribs back into place. I was back at work the next day.'

ON THE LAND

We have always had a comforting affection for this great, wide, brown land — warts and all. There are certainly extremes with massive, red dust deserts, raging rivers that snake their way across plains and gullies, towering mountain ranges, huge inland lakes that appear and disappear at will, and jagged coasts with either sandy beaches or treacherous drops into wild ocean.

This is the land that explorers like Burke and Wills, Ludwig Leichhardt and William Wentworth traversed, mapped and stood in awe of its immense size. It is the land that has seen so many changes from humble and dark beginnings as a penal settlement to the land where hopeful diggers could 'pick up lumps of gold on the streets'. It was the land that allowed us to cock our colonial-born noses at Mother England as we rode home on the backs of sheep and cattle. It was the land that saw railways and river boats link town to town, and city to city. The land that boasted coal mines, factories and fisheries. It was also the land that allowed our early wordsmiths and poetical dreamers such as Henry Lawson, Will Ogilvie and A.B. 'Banjo' Paterson to link the earth to our national soul.

REGULATIONS FOR COCKIES

Rule 1: No cocky shall speak disrespectfully of the AWU, the Labor party, Andrew Fisher, the cook, the shearers or the shedhands.

Rule 2: Before coming onto the board, all cockies shall have their whiskers trimmed, as the shearers consider that some cockies' whiskers are as dangerous as barbed wire entanglements.

Rule 3: In the advent of a shearer or shedhand asking a cocky for tobacco or matches, the cocky shall instantly produce them and shall stand with a respectful attitude till the said shearer or shedhand has filled or lit his pipe.

Rule 4: The cocky shall not stand in front of a shearer or shedhand for more than five minutes.

Rule 5: All cockies are expected to treat shearers and shedhands to whisky.

Rule 6: Cockies shall not (under any circumstance) talk about the land tax, scarcity of labour, immigration, or the country being ruined.

Rule 7: The cocky must not assume any superior airs and he shall not call himself the 'backbone of the country'.

Rule 8: In the event of a shearer requiring a drink of tea, his comb and cutter box, his pipe filled, or any other service whatsoever, the cocky shall spring off the balls of his feet and do it at once.

THOSE CATHOLIC BASTARDS

A station owner up near central Queensland had a ringer working for him named Jacky Quart-Pot.

One day Jacky said: 'Boss, I'm leaving to cut the prickly pear.'

The station boss replied: 'Fine, Jack, how long do you plan to be away?'

'Oh, about six months, Boss.'

Well, Jacky Quart-Pot returned to the station about three weeks later and when the boss asked why he had returned so soon, Jacky replied: 'No work up there now, Boss, those Catholic bastards (cactoblastis) they kill 'em already.'

A GOOD CAR FOR THE BUSH

The grazier had struck it rich with seven good seasons in a row, and to celebrate he had purchased a brand new Rolls-Royce 'Silver Cloud'. He took it back to the local agent for its first service and the sales manager greeted him like a long lost friend.

'And are you satisfied with the car, sir?'

The grazier looked at the man and nodded. 'Yep, it's a mighty fine vehicle and I particularly like the glass partition between the driver's seat and the rear 'cause it stops the bloody cows from licking the back of me head!'

SPUDS

The new chum had been looking for work without luck when he spied an advertisement in the rural newspaper for a job as a potato picker with a spud cocky of Bungaree. He applied in person.

'Yair,' indicated the farmer, who had a face like a dirty potato, 'you can have the job if yer want it. A quid a week and tucker, sleep in the cow shed, we gets up at 4.00 a.m. and knock orf at 7.00 p.m., second Sunday orf.'

The new chum scratched his head. 'Look 'ere, I think you'd be better off finding the bloke who planted the potatoes — he'd have a better chance of knowing where to find them.'

NOT SO SMART

The farmer's daughter was young, attractive and a pretty good hand with the cattle. As it turned out, her father had taken on a couple of bricklayers from the city to build a new shearer's hut and, like a lot of city people, they thought that all country people were dim-witted. On their third morning there, they spied the young girl and thought they'd have a bit of a joke.

'Hey, Miss! Do you know if anyone in the area has a rooster that lays eggs?'

The girl looked over at the two men and smiled.

'No, sorry, I wouldn't have a clue about that, but Father told me at breakfast that he had brought two galahs from the city who thought they could lay bricks.'

I'LL BUY THAT

The city slicker was determined to buy a horse at the monthly stock auction and waited patiently as each horse was offered and sold. Halfway through the auction, they led in an old and obviously clapped-out beast that looked like it should have been headed for the knackery. The city bloke started bidding enthusiastically until the surprised auctioneer slammed the hammer down.

'Sold!' he announced.

The squatter seated next to the city slicker couldn't help himself, and leant over to the man and politely asked: 'What do you plan to do with him?'

The city slicker, looking as pleased as Punch, announced: 'Race him!'

The squatter looked at the old horse and then back at the city slicker.

'Yes, you should win!'

NOT DONALD

There had been a terrible accident at the railway station. Donald the general hand had been run over by a train and the only part of his body that didn't get mangled was his head. When the time came for the squatter to identify the body, the coroner held up Donald's poor head and asked whether this man was Donald Mackay?

The squatter looked at it for a full five minutes and answered: 'No, definitely not, Donald was much taller.'

THE COCKY OF BUNGAREE

Now all you blokes take my advice and do your daily toil.
And don't go out to Bungaree to work on the chocolate soil.
For the days they are so long, my boys, they'll break your
   heart in two.
And if ever you work for Cocky Bourke, you very soon
   will know.

Oh, we used to go to bed, you know, a little bit after dark.
The room we used to sleep in, it was just like Noah's Ark.
There were dogs and rats and mice and cats and pigs and
   poulteree.
I'll never forget the time we had while down in Bungaree.

On the thirsty Monday morning, sure, to work I had to go.
The noble Cocky says to me: 'Get up! You're rather slow.'
The moon was shining gloriously, and the stars were out,
   you see.
And I thought before the sun would rise I'd die in Bungaree.

Oh, he called me to my supper at half past eight or nine.
He called me to my breakfast before the sun could shine.
And after tea was over, all with a merry laugh.
The bloody old Cocky says to me: 'We'll cut a bit of chaff.'

Now when you are chaff-cutting, boys, isn't it a spell?
'Yes, by Jove,' says I, 'it is, and it's me that knows it well!'
For many of those spells with me they disagree.
For I hate the bloody night work that they do on Bungaree.

(Traditional song from the singing of Simon McDonald)

SAVE TIME

Way out beyond the Black Stump, one of the locals was making his monthly trip down to the nearest railway junction and was amazed to see a gang of construction workers putting down a new branch line. Stopping his truck, he asked for the engineer to find out what was going on.

'This new line will change your life, mate,' he was told. 'It will go right up to your area — more or less to your door.'

The farmer stared in amazement.

'How long does it take you to get down to the station now?' enquired the engineer.

'Four days, if the weather's fine,' replied the farmer.

'Well, rest assured that when we've finished it will only take you a day to get your produce down here and you'll get home all in one day.'

'Struth!' declared the farmer, as he dubiously scratched his chin. 'What the hell will I do with the other three days?'

A BIG STATION

A shearer was out west looking for work when he came across a huge mob of sheep which seemed to stretch for miles. It took him an hour and a half to get to the head of them, where he saw this bloke sitting on a horse.

'Good day,' the shearer said. 'Are you with these sheep?'

'Well, yes and no,' came the reply. 'I'm with the dogs and I've got fifty-three of the devils.'

The shearer was eager for work and pressed the drover for information about his station.

'Well,' drawled the drover, 'they belong to an outfit called the Burraweena Pastoral Company and, as far as I know, they are always shearing to keep up with the mob.'

'Strike a light!' exclaimed the shearer. 'It must be a bloody big shed.'

'Oh, it's a big shed alright. I don't know too much about it except that they have forty cooks just to cook for their cooks. Yes, it's a pretty big shed,' the drover concluded.

CROWS

The new chum was innocent,
Or so the story goes,
He did just what the boss had said,
And stoned the flamin' crows.

If there is one sound immediately identifiable with the Australian outback, it is more likely to be that of the crow rather than the kookaburra. The crow's piercing cry is ever present as you travel through the bush — especially where there are grain-rich fields ready and waiting for the looting. Understandably, farmers learn to hate the sound of the crow.

My old friend and noted oral historian, Wendy Lowenstein, recorded 'The Three Black Crows' in 1969 from Jack 'Speargrass' Guard of Georgetown, Queensland. The song is an Australian version of a very old ballad known as the 'Twa Corbies'. In the original version, the ravens pick out the eyes of a knight but this version has a definite Australian flavour with the crows picking out the eyes of a dead horse.

THE THREE BLACK CROWS

Now three black crows sat in a tree,
They were black as black could be,
Crrrk, Crrrk, Crrrk.

Said one black crow unto the other,
'Where shall we dine today, dear brother?'
Crrrk, Crrrk, Crrrk.

On yonder hill's an old grey mare,
I think, my friends, we shall dine there,
Crrrk, Arrrk, Arrrk.

They perched upon her high backbone,
And picked her eyes out one by one,
Crrrk, Crrrk, Crrrk.

Said one old crow unto the other,
'Isn't she a tough old bugger?'
Arrrk, Arrrk, Arrrk.

Up came the squatter with his gun,
And shot them all excepting one,
Crrrrk, Crrrk, Crrrk.

Now that one black crow got such a fright,
It turned from black right into white,
Crrrk, Crrrk, Crrrk.

And that is why you'll often see,
A single white crow sitting on a tree,
Crrrk, Crrrk, Crrrk.

THAT FARMER HATES CROWS!

It had been very dry out the back of Woop Woop, and there was this crow which had been reduced to a scrawny assembly of crow bones with hardly a feather to his name. He was a miserable-looking bird.

Enough was enough, he decided. And, as he'd heard stories about the 'pastures of plenty' in the Murrumbidgee Irrigation Area, he vowed, then and there, that he would relocate.

Well, he set forth on his big journey and eventually he reached the outskirts of Griffith, where he rested on a big tree branch. As he huffed and puffed, he glanced sideways and sitting right next to him was the plumpest, blackest, most handsome crow he had ever seen.

'G'day,' the shiny one said. 'Where the hell have you come from? You look horrible — all skin and bones!'

Gathering his crow breath the visitor explained his background and ambition to regain his feathers and sheen.

'Look friend,' offered the shiny one. 'You're most welcome to join me here on this farm, it's a real lark and a great life for any crow. Every day, the farmer comes out and feeds that bull over there with the best oats, maize and lucerne, and after a few hours the bull drops 'meadow cakes' and I simply fly down and eat all I want. The only warning I'll give you is that the farmer really hates crows, has a thing about them, so absolutely no crow noises.'

Well, this all sounded too good to be true and, of course, our outback mate accepted the hospitality. After a few months he, too, had become big and fat, feathered and black. It was indeed a glorious lifestyle by any crow standards.

One day, full of oats, maize and lucerne, he flew back to the branch as happy as Larry. Pleasure took hold of him, and he simply couldn't resist a loud crowing call of: 'Ccrraaak.'

He was in mid-crow when the farmer raced out with his rifle and 'Bang!' shot him stone dead.

The moral of this story is: If you're full of bullshit — keep your mouth shut!

LOOK OUT FOR THE CROWS

The new chum had just landed in the bush and his boss sent him out to check the paddocks with firm instructions to 'look out for the crows'.

When he returned after his first day on the land, the farmer asked him if he'd seen any crows.

'Yes,' said the green new chum.

'You scared the buggers off?'

'No, sir, I thought they were yours!'

CADGERS

The economic depressions of the 1890s and 1930s sent many Australian men and women into the bush to 'carry the swag'. The government, in an attempt to control the unemployment situation, introduced a sustenance program whereby men had to travel a designated distance in order to be eligible for the dole. It created a nation of 'road travellers' who were known as: swagmen, tramps, bagmen, hatters, bums, hoboes and sundowners. Survival depended on how crafty and clever you were, and some of the cadging antics of the travelling people produced a vast number of yarns, poems, songs and lore.

Farmers were generally sympathetic to the swaggies, and it was customary for a standard ration handout known as the 'five doubler' or the 'five, two and double-half' (the 'doubler'). It was five pounds of flour, two pounds of beef, half a pound of sugar and half a pound of tea. They say in the really tough times, they still got five, two and double half — five minutes to get off the property, two reasons why you could be had up for trespassing, half a yard start on the dog and only half a chance to explain yourself!

The sundowners were the least welcome, as they were the ones that arrived at the homestead door at sundown in the hope of avoiding the usual wood-chopping or other farm work usually done in exchange for rations.

I recorded Bart Saggers in 1974, and he told me how he had been a 'professional swagman' right through the Depression and he was universally known as 'The Great Australian Bite'. He told me there was even a Swagman's Union with its own set of rules.

1. No member to be over 100 years of age.
2. Each member to pay one pannikin of flour entrance fee. Members who do not care about paying it will be admitted free.

3. No member to carry swags weighing over ten pounds.

4. Each member to possess three complete sets of tucker-bags, each set to consist of nine bags.

5. No member to pass any station, farm, homestead or boundary rider's hut without tapping and obtaining rations and handouts.

6. No member to allow himself to be bitten by a sheep. If a sheep bites a member, he must immediately turn it into mutton.

7. Members who defame a good cook or pay a fine when run in shall be expelled by the union.

8. No member is allowed to solicit baking powder, tea, flour, sugar or tobacco from a fellow unionist.

9. Any member found without at least two sets of bags filled with tucker will be fined.

10. No member to look for or accept work of any description. Members found working will be expelled.

11. No member to walk more than five miles per day if rations can be found.

12. No member to tramp on a Sunday at any price.

YOU'LL HAVE TO USE THE AXE

The sundowner arrived at the homestead just as the sun was setting. He knew that it would be unlikely that he would be asked to work in the dark.

He knocked on the door and politely asked the station owner if he could spare a loaf of bread.

'You'll have to use the axe,' came the reply.

The sundowner, an experienced Roads Scholar, looked the station owner in the eye.

'Oh that won't be necessary, I'll just soak it in me tea.'

A GOOD MATCH

The old-timer made his way up to the station shed, where he approached the hard-faced station boss.

'I wuz wondering where I should go to request me rations?'

The farmer turned to the swaggie with a look that would scare crows and proceeded to tell the man that he wouldn't get any rations from anyone on this property and, further more, if he didn't get off the property in five minutes, he'd be thrown off.

The old swaggie gave the farmer a distasteful look and nodded his head.

'Is that right, Sir? In that case, you leave me no option than to refer you to my lawyers.'

The farmer looked back at the man with a sneer and sarcastically asked: 'And who might your lawyers be?'

'Bryant and May,' the swaggie said, smiling knowingly.

He got his rations immediately!

A QUICK ONE

Bill the shearer's cook was well known as a cadger, so when he bailed up Smithy the local off-duty copper, he tried his best to strike up a conversation.

'What about a quick one?' asked Bill.

'Don't drink,' replied Smithy.

'Have a cigarette then?'

'No, thanks, don't smoke.'

'Ever had any headaches?' enquired Bill.

'Yes, pretty often these days,' replied Smithy.

'Just as I thought! Your halo's too bloody tight!'

A LITTLE BIT OF THE IRISH

The Irish swagman had a way with words, and when on the cadge he'd make his way to the cookhouse and sprout forthwith: 'Could I be having a drink of water or tea, please, and God bless your cow, and I'm that hungry I don't know where I'm going to sleep tonight, for the want of a smoke.'

THE GRASS IS GREENER

Swaggies use every trick in the book to get a handout, but one knot-carrier I met was the kingpin of all cadgers. He used to embarrass the lady of the house into generous rations. One day, he met his match. He had lazily walked through the property, carefully closing the gates after him, and he stood at the front door and loudly knocked twice.

The station owner's wife opened the door and suspiciously eyed the sundowner.

'Yes?' she enquired.

He took a sweeping bow.

'Good evening, Missus, and a lovely one it is, too. I wuz wondering if youse could spare me some margarine?'

As he delivered these words, he thrust a hardened, old, dried-out cow's turd towards her. 'Some margarine, Missus?'

She looked at him and curtly grabbed the 'meadow cake' and tossed it away, saying: 'Oh, you poor old traveller. Don't you worry. You go around to the back of the house, there's some fresh ones there!'

ST GEORGE AND THE DRAGON

Swagmen needed to be quick if they were to be successful cadgers, but sometimes the odds are simply too much. One old Roads Scholar found himself in unknown parts in front of the Saint George and The Dragon Hotel, so he made his way to the rear of the pub to ask for rations. He knocked politely and the back door was opened by a large woman who immediately commenced yelling at him like a harpy.

'You good-for-nothing, lazy loafer.' She added that if he was expecting a handout, he had better get moving before she called the police.

The sundowner stood silently listening and when she was finished, he looked up and said: 'I was wondering if I could have a word with George?'

KICK THE BILLY

You meet some odd sorts when you travel the backblocks and the 'hatters' (as in 'mad hatters') were the most eccentric. I remember once when I had been droving in far Western Australia. I had set up my campfire by the road and was just about to boil the billy and make some dinner when an old hatter arrived carrying a swag. I gestured that he could join me if he liked but he ignored me and started to set up his own campfire a little further up the track.

I watched him as he settled down and then I saw him take a large billy can from his swag and then, of all things, a small dog. He set them both up by the fire and they didn't move as he took out a grimy old pack of cards, which he started to shuffle.

As time moved on, he dealt the billy can five cards, the dog five cards and then five for himself. He sat there studying the cards and I couldn't help but wander over and silently watch this unusual poker game. The billy can had a pair of tens, the dog had a pair of Jacks and the hatter a pair of deuces. Patiently, the hatter took the discarded cards and dealt each player three new cards.

Picking up his own cards, he saw that they hadn't improved. Then, all of a sudden, he leapt to his feet and angrily booted the billy can into the darkness, shouting after it: 'That'll teach you to look at the dog's hand, you sneaky bastard!'

ROAD DIRECTIONS

Completely bushwhacked on an outback road somewhere past Woop Woop, a tourist slammed on the brakes and pulled his car over to stop beside a swaggie who was trudging along in the scorching midday sun.

'I say,' called the driver, 'can you give me the directions to the next town?'

'Yeah,' replied the swaggie, as he wiped a flow of grimy sweat from his brow. 'You turn right at the next crossroad, travel about ten miles until you spot a big shed, turn right again until you see a big gum tree, then turn right again until you come to a train line, then turn right.'

An hour later, the same car came bouncing down the same road and the car once again pulled over to where the swaggie was seated, resting under a gum tree.

'I never could follow directions,' said the tourist. 'Could you do me a big favour and travel with me so you could point out the way?'

'Certainly,' said the swaggie, climbing in. 'Just drive straight ahead. You're lucky mate, sometimes I send fellows like you around the track about three or four times before they offer me a lift!'

COCKEYE BURNS' CURRANT BUNS

We had a bloke with us called Cockeye Burns and he fancied himself as a bit of a cook. He once made us currant buns and we were all sitting around the campfire hoeing into them when someone commented that the currants were 'as hard as nails'.

'Did you soak the currants?' another enquired.

'No, why would I want to have done that?' Cockeye replied.

'Well, they're very hard and obviously not cooked and, besides, they taste bitter.'

Cockeye Burns gave us all a long glance and explained how he had picked them up from the shed floor where food scraps often fell during the unpacking after delivery. What he hadn't told us was that the sheep had also discovered the currants and what Cockeye had picked up was a mixture of currants and sheep droppings. We never allowed him to cook again!

DOGS

Dogs have played a special role in the Australian tradition. In a land where workers spent endless days, and often weeks, riding the boundary fences, waiting for the shearing season to open, or riding their bullock drays through endless forests, the dog has been a true mate. It has also been an equal working partner, jumping from sheep's back to sheep's back, up and down onto the bullock dray and yelping at the heels of stubborn cattle. They come in all shapes and sizes and usually end up with generic names such as: Bluey, Piddling Pete or Red.

> *Me and my dog*
> *We travel the bush,*
> *In weather cold or hot.*
> *Me and my dog,*
> *We don't give a stuff,*
> *If we get any work or not.*
> (Old drinking toast)

In folklore, dogs seem to take on supernatural powers. They talk, they perform extraordinary deeds and they like the occasional drink of beer.

THE DOGS' MEETING

The dogs they held a party,
They came from near and far,
Some they came by aeroplane,
And some by motorcar.
And when they arrived,
Each one had a look,
Each had to take his arsehole off,
And hang it on a hook.

And hardly were they seated there,
Each mother, son and sire,
When a dirty little yellow dog
Began to holler: 'Fire!'
Out they rushed in panic,
They didn't stop to look,
Each dog he grabbed an arsehole
From off the nearest hook.

And that's the reason why you see,
When walking down the street,
Each dog will stop and swap a smell
With every dog he meets,
And that's the reason why a dog
Will leave a good fat bone,
To go an sniff an arsehole
In case he finds his own.

(Traditional ditty)

COLD NOSE

Ted the Queensland drover was visiting town and doing his best to sink a few coldies when, as usual, the pub talk turned to dogs.

'See that there kelpie of mine, he's the ugliest, scrawniest mongrel in the entire bloody state and I'll bet there's not a dog that'll come anywhere near him.'

The crowd of hard-nosed bushies had heard this sort of exaggerated claim before and doubt was written all over their assembled faces.

The drover looked at them and added: 'Soon as a dog spots him, they put their tails between their legs and they're off.'

'Must be one hell of a fighter,' said one of the doubtful.

'No, he's no fighter,' said the drover, 'but he's got the coldest bloody nose in the Southern Hemisphere.'

RICH MEN AFTER ALL

I was up in Cootamundra when a swagman and his fleabag dog came into the bar. It was obvious that he didn't have enough dosh to buy a beer, so I was about to shout him when in waltzes another swaggie and his dog. I turned around and, for conversation, told the first swaggie that he had a mighty fine-looking dog.

'This dog,' explained the swag carrier, 'has to be the best dog in the whole of the country and I wouldn't sell him for a thousand dollars.'

By this stage the second swaggie, looking just as parched and broke, took a look at his own dog and joined the conversation.

'Personally, I wouldn't take two thousand dollars for my faithful canine friend.'

The exasperated barman looked at both the swaggies and couldn't hold himself back from saying: 'You wouldn't read about it, would ya! Two men with over three thousand dollars worth of dogs and not a brass razoo to buy a beer!'

TILBURY'S DOG

The drover named Tilbury had a talking dog that had travelled with him right across Australia. He never let anyone know about this talking dog until one day, a swag-carrier overheard the two of them having a conversation.

'How long have you had this dog?' the swaggie asked.

'Three years,' replied the drover.

'Holy dooley! Why haven't you told anyone else about your talking dog?'

The drover shrugged and whispered: 'I thought he'd outgrow it by now.'

WHAT NOT TO CALL YOUR DOG

The stockman had landed himself in gaol and was attempting to explain his story to the booking clerk.

'It's a long story but it all started when I named my dog "Sex" — the name stuck and proved to be the only name it would respond to.

'The first problem was when I went to the Shire Council to register for a dog licence. I told the clerk I wanted a licence for Sex but he just looked at me and said he wouldn't mind one, too. I insisted that this one was for a dog. He said he didn't care what she looked like, so I tried to explain that I've had Sex since I was nine years old. He just looked at me, shaking his head.

'When I got married and went on my honeymoon I had to take the dog with me. I told the receptionist that I wanted the bridal suite for the wife and me and a special room for Sex. The receptionist said that every room in the hotel was for sex so I had to explain that Sex keeps me awake at night. He just nodded his head in agreement.

'Last month, I entered Sex into an obedience contest but before I knew it, Sex had bolted. The judge asked me why I was standing around so I explained that I had intended to have Sex in the competition. He stared at me and said if he'd known, he'd have sold tickets to the show. But you don't understand, I protested, I wanted to have Sex on the television news. He seemed upset with that and called me a show-off.

'When my wife and I separated, we went to the divorce court to fight for custody of the dog and I told the judge that I'd had Sex before I got married. The judge said he had, too.

'Last night, Sex ran off again and I spent hours looking for him. That's when the police officer asked me what I was doing roaming the streets at 4.00 a.m. and I told him I was looking for Sex. That's why I'm in here.'

TALENTED DOG

Another story from the hard times tells of a meeting of two swag-carriers up near the town of Bellingen. They both had done some hard tramping, and time had come to set up camp down by the river and boil up the billy. They sat around the campfire with their dogs and, as campfire talk commands, they got to talking about one of the few subjects that they had in common — their dogs! As the evening wore on, so did the conversation as each man attempted to 'up the ante' on the other, especially in regards to the talent and ability of their respective dogs. The conversation was becoming more and more heated and was definitely headed towards the status of an argument!

'I swear that my dog is the smartest bloody animal in the state of New South Wales,' one declared.

'That's nothing,' declared the other, as he matched story for story. Finally, one of the men jumped to his feet in disgust. 'Listen here, cobber, I don't want to hear another word of your bullshit. If I can prove to you that my dog is the smartest dog in the entire country, will you give me five quid in the morning?'

The challenge was laid and the bet accepted — the dog would prepare breakfast in the morning or he'd pay the fiver.

At the first hint of morning sun, the kelpie mutt jumped to his feet and raced off into the scrub. Fifteen minutes later, the dog surprised the swaggie by returning and carefully dropping two fresh farm eggs on the sand next to the fire. Grabbing a forked stick, the dog poked and prodded the embers until the fire caught alight again. Next, the dog grabbed the billy and raced down to the river, where it filled the can with fresh water. He made his way back to the camp, where he used the forked stick to place the billy can on the heat. He gave the other dog a sneering glance and sat back to wait for the billy to boil.

As the water began to boil, the dog carefully picked up the two eggs and ever so gently plonked them into the billy. He sat back with his back as straight as an ironbark and waited for exactly three minutes, when he quickly picked up the forked stick and removed the billy from the fire.

By this time, the challenged swaggie had given up the contest and was staring with his mouth wide open. As he stared in amazement, the dog performed a triple somersault and landed on his two front paws and remained there with his tail pointed to the heavens.

'The bet's off!' yelled the panicking swaggie, his thoughts placed directly on his precious five quid. 'The bet's called off on the grounds that the dog is clearly insane.'

The old swaggie who owned the dog had said nothing all the time his dog had performed the routine.

'The bet's on, mate. The dog is quite sane and, if you are referring to his last little performance, I would remind you that he is well aware of the fact that I haven't got an egg cup!'

A DOG THAT LIKES A BEER

Dogs that like a beer or three aren't that unusual in the bush, but when Cleary waltzed into a local pub and saw a swaggie and his kelpie enjoying long glasses of the amber fluid, he couldn't but help make a remark.

'Your dog seems to enjoy a beer.' He nodded as he watched the dog, beer in paw, seated at the bar.

'Yeah, he's a drinker from way back.'

Cleary took another admiring look and added: 'Yes, just like a human.'

The swaggie nodded. 'Yeah, too right, you just watch the bastard disappear when it's his bloody shout.'

A CHAMPION SHEEP DOG

Bush workers love to tell stories about their dogs and, one suspects, the dogs enjoy telling tales about their masters. One of the most popular stories concerns the exploits of a ginger mutt who had been sent out by the station boss to bring in 100 lost sheep. The dog returned two days later with ninety-nine sheep, and the skin of the sheep he had used as rations. He was a champion sheep dog, that one.

PIDDLING PETE

A farmer's dog came into town,
His Christian name was Pete,
A noble pedigree had he,
To see him was a treat.

And as he trotted down the street,
'Twas beautiful to see,
His work on every corner,
His work on every tree.

He watered every gateway, too,
And never missed a post,
'Cause piddling was his specialty,
And piddling was his boast.

The city curs looked on amazed,
With deep and jealous rage,
To see a simple country dog,
The piddler of the age.

Some thought that he a king might be,
Beneath his tail a rose,
So every dog drew near to him,
And sniffed him up the nose.

They sniffed him over one by one,
They sniffed him two by two,
And noble Pete with high disdain,
Stood still till they were through.

They called for champion piddlers,
From all around the town,
Pete only smiled, and polished off
The ablest, white or brown.

Then Pete went piddling merrily,
With hind leg lifted high,
While most were lifting legs in bluff,
And piddling mostly dry.

And just to show the whole shebang,
He didn't give a damn,
He walked into a grocer's shop,
And piddled on a ham.

He piddled in a mackerel keg,
He piddled on the floor,
And when the grocer kicked him out,
He piddled through the door.

Then Pete did freehand piddling
With fancy flirts and flits,
With double dip, and gimlet twist,
And all the latest hits.

And when Pete at last left town,
They asked what did defeat us,
But what they didn't know was that
Poor Pete had diabetes.

(Anonymous poem)

METAL WORKER

A swaggie walks into a country pub with his mangy old dog following close at his well-worn heels. The knot-carrier takes a seat and the dog sits silently at his feet.

'Sorry, mate, you're welcome to have a drink but your dog will have to wait outside. No dog's allowed in the hotel by the management's orders.'

The swaggie was about to leave when he spotted a kelpie sitting under a table chewing on a piece of wood.

'Well, what in thunder's name is that?' he said, pointing to the table.

'Oh, him,' responded the barman. 'He's got a special dispensation because he's a wood carver. Give him a piece of timber and he'll chew at it until he's carved a figure or statue.'

The old swaggie eyed the dog and then the barman.

'That's all very impressive, but my dog's a metal worker,' he offered.

'Bull dust!' exclaimed the barman.

The swaggie took another long, distasteful look at the barman and said: 'Well, you go and get a piece of steel about eighteen inches long and we'll see about that.'

The barman, exasperated, disappeared and returned with a piece of gas pipe and asked: 'Now, what do I do with this?'

'Shove it up his arse,' instructed the swaggie.

The barman snapped back: 'How can he make anything like that?'

'He'll either make a spring for your nuts or a bolt for the door,' said the swaggie with a smile.

BEER CHASER

A drover's dog went into a pub and casually ordered a beer.

'And put in a nip of brandy,' added the dog with a knowing smile.

The barman mixed the beer and brandy concoction as requested and silently placed the glass in front of the dog.

'I suppose you think it's peculiar,' the dog commented, 'that I should walk in here and ask for a beer mixed with brandy?'

'Cripes, no!' said the barman. 'I drink it like that myself.'

A GAME OF CHESS

One of those commercial traveller blokes was driving out in the backblocks when he spied a swagman's campsite by the side of the road. Pulling over, he couldn't help but notice that the swagman had a chess board set up on an upturned orange crate and sitting opposite him was a red kelpie. The commercial traveller watched in amazement as the swaggie and the dog were concentrating on the game.

'That's a mighty clever dog you've got there,' the traveller offered.

'I dunno about that,' growled the swagman indignantly. 'I beat him as often as he beats me.'

BUSH PUBS AND THE DEMON DRINK

Hotel dining rooms seem to attract a steady flow of folklore. Maybe this is because old country pubs were such a focus for both travellers and locals in a climate where itinerant workers were the labour muscles of the country. The food was generally unbelievably awful, the service insulting and the company far from grand.

PUB TABLE (Or how 2 pints equals 30 days)

2 pints = 1 quart
1 quart = 1 argument
1 argument = 1 fight
1 fight = 1 copper
1 copper = 1 arrest
1 arrest = 1 judge
1 judge = 30 days

* * *

The German likes his beer,
The Pommy likes his half-and-half,
Because it brings good cheer.
The Scotsman likes his whisky,
The Irishman his hot.
The Aussie has no national drink,
So he drinks the bloody lot!

One could be excused for thinking yesterday's Australians, especially our bush workers, were world-class boozers. While we consumed a great deal of liquor of every description, it would be fairer to say that we lived by the maxim: work hard, play hard.

In most cases, alcohol was not part of working life, and since so much of our outback work was seasonal and contractual, there were obvious controls on when and how the men could drink. When they finished their season and received their pay cheques, they usually headed for home or the closest shanty. There are horror stories about men being on a spree and having their cheques 'cut down' by unscrupulous landlords and landladies.

The practice of 'lambing down' the workers was widespread, with the thirsty shearer or drover handing over his pay cheque with the instruction: 'Let me know when I've cut it out.' Sometimes, weeks later, the man struggled up in a stupor, often induced by rum that had been 'strengthened' by tobacco juice and other dubious additions.

One landlady was famous for settling the remainder of cheques by baking her cheque in the oven so that, days later, as the man rode off into the sunset, the cheque would simply disintegrate in the saddlebag.

They're sleeping on verandahs, they're lounging on the sofas,
And they finish off their spree, they're ordered off as loafers,
Their money's gone, their friends have flown,
And at their disappearing, they give three cheers for the riverbend,
And jog along 'till shearing.

(Traditional song)

The folklore related to drink in Australia is varied and e7xtremely colourful. One of my favourites is a parody on one of Australia's best-loved country songs, 'The Pub With No Beer'. The songwriter of the parody changed the story to produce a hilarious situation that will be familiar to city and country person alike. It was printed anonymously in *Singabout* for the Bush Music Club in 1961.

THE PUB WITH NO DIKE

I'll tell you a story, it happened to me,
A new pub had opened and the beer, it flowed free,
I'd had several drinks and was full of wild cheer,
Mother Nature came calling and I went for a walk.

There were blokes going out there were blokes coming in,
And the racket they made was a hell of a din,
I spoke to a swaggie we all know as Ike,
And sadly he told me: 'The pub's got no dike.'

So I wandered out back in the chilly night air,
And saw about twenty more blokes standing there,
Some yodelling, some cursing, but say what you like,
They wouldn't have been there if the pub had a dike.

Then I got quite a scare and my heart gave a thump,
I thought Bill the blacksmith was only a stump,
He got up and cursed me and said: 'Dirty dog!
Why don't you go elsewhere to run off your grog.'

'Twas then the top button broke off my pants,
And they fell down and tripped me in a nest of green ants,
I yahooed and yakkied and boy, did I hike,
I couldn't care less if that pub had a dike.

I ran back inside over bottles and kegs,
My trousers like hobbles, still tripping my legs,
My mates poured some whiskey where my rump it was hot,
And the old spinster barmaid dropped dead on the spot.

Then a big drunken cowboy, eyes bulging like buns,
Said: 'I'll fix those ants, boy! And drew both his guns,
The first shot he fired rang out through the night,
And the sting of the bullets hurt worse than the bite.

I got such a fright that I ran from the hall
And jumped on my push-bike, no trousers at all,
And vowed I'd make sure as I pedalled that bike,
That the next pub I go to really does have a dike.

* * *

Here's to the bull that roams in the wood,
That does the heifer a great deal of good,
If it wasn't for him and his big red rod,
What would we do for beef, by God!

(Traditional toast)

WHY THE HELL DO WE DRINK?

We drink for joy and become miserable.

We drink for sociability and become argumentative.

We drink for sophistication and become obnoxious.

We drink to help us sleep and awake exhausted.

We drink for exhilaration and end up depressed.

We drink to gain confidence and become afraid.

We drink to make conversation and become incoherent.

We drink to diminish our problems and see them multiply.

SHOCKING GRAFFITI

A woman who had never been in the bush before was finding things very different from what she was used to in the city. On her first visit to a country hotel, she came out of the Ladies with a look of horror on her face.

As she was leaving the hotel, she said to the waitress: 'Please tell the owner of this joint that I found your graffiti in very bad taste.'

'I will,' said the waitress, 'but next time, I suggest you try the spaghetti.'

ANOTHER DOZEN

The hotel offered a very limited menu — stewed galah or stewed mountain goat.

The young bush worker knew enough about the tough old galah not to go that way, so he pointed to the goat.

'Nar, can't 'ave the goat, mate,' rasped the waitress, 'that's reserved for the boarders.'

Not wanting to chew on the nigh impossible, he asked the waitress for 'some boiled eggs, please, Miss'.

When the waitress returned, she plonked down a dozen newly boiled eggs.

'I can't eat that many eggs, I only want two,' protested the young man.

'Look, love, if yer can't find a couple of good ones in that lot let me know and I'll boil yer up another dozen.'

BORE WATER

It was out near White Rock, beyond Wilcannia, and the travelling salesman had been on the road for quite some time. He was destined to spend three days in this area, and was staying at the only hotel in the excuse for a town. On the first morning he headed to the dining room for breakfast, where he was welcomed by the young waitress, shown to a table and handed a copy of the hotel menu.

'Miss, I'll have the lamb chops and eggs, please.'

'Sorry, Sir,' came the reply, 'we're out of lamb chops but cook tells me we have some delicious pork chops.'

He ate his breakfast and headed out to sell his wares. He returned at lunch time, where he was once again handed the menu.

'I'll have the corned beef salad, please, Miss.'

'Sorry, Sir, cook says that the corned beef is off today but he can do you a nice cold pickled pork salad.'

Lunch over, the salesman leaves to do his door-knocking job. That evening after a beer or two, he headed for the hotel dining room where, once again, he is met by the waitress and handed the menu.

'I'll have the roast beef, please.'

'Sorry, Sir, we haven't got any beef but cookie has done a very nice roast pork.'

The salesman was getting quite upset about all this salty pork but refrained from an outburst and said: 'Alright, I'll have the roast pork, Miss. I'll also have a glass of water.'

After a few mouthfuls of the salty pork, he reached for the glass of water and swallowed half of it before the taste hit him. Spitting the water out, he yelled at the waitress: 'What the hell is this water? It's as salty as the Dead Sea.'

The waitress turned quite red as she attempted to apologise. 'I'm terribly sorry, Sir, I should have told you but, because of the drought, we only have bore water.'

'Bore water!' exclaimed the salesman. 'You certainly don't waste much of the pig around here!'

COCKROACHES

The itinerant shearer booked into a country pub and was signing the registry when he noticed a large black cockroach watching him.

'Strike me dead!' exclaimed the shearer. 'I've seen lots of old pubs and I've seen lots of cockroaches, but it's the first time I've seen one bothered enough to read my room number!'

BLOWFLIES

An American staying at a country pub had been trying to pluck up the courage to confront the publican about the number of blowflies in the outhouse. After a couple of days, he collared the licensee and made his complaint.

'What time do yer go in there?'

'Oh, about eleven o'clock,' replied his guest.

The licensee nodded with understanding. 'You should go about twelve o'clock,' he said. 'They'll all be in the dining room about then.'

Here's to you as good as you are,
And here's to me as bad as I am,
And as good as you are,
And as bad as I am,
I'm as good as you are,
As bad as I am.

(**Traditional toast**)

DRINK THAT!

In the far outback where pubs are few, a parched drover wandered into a local shanty. The bar was empty except for a seedy-looking fellow staring at a long glass of evil-looking black fluid. Next thing the drover knew, he had a rifle shoved into his ribs and the lone drinker was shouting: 'Drink that!'

The drover gulped the vile liquid down and stared back at the cove.

'Crook stuff, isn't it?' the drinker said. 'But it's all we've got.'

He ordered another glass, handed the drover the rifle, and said: 'Okay, my turn. Now you hold that gun on me while I drink.'

ALL AROUND THE TOWN

Bill the shearer was on a bender and staggered into the bar.

'Give us a drink, cobber.'

The barman took one look at him and apologised, telling him that he couldn't possibly serve him alcohol while he was in that state.

Bill left by the side door and reappeared via the back door. He staggered up to the bar and demanded a beer but the barman just looked at him and, once again, apologised, saying that he couldn't possibly serve him in his present state.

Bill wheeled out the front door and almost immediately reappeared from the salon door.

'Give us a drink, matey-o,' he slurred.

'Look, mate,' threatened the barman. 'I've told you once, I've told you twice and I've told you three times — you're too drunk, get out of here.'

The boozer started at him in amazement.

'Strike me pink! What'd'ya do — work in every bloody pub in town!'

HE KNOWS WHEN HE'S HAD ENOUGH

Two shearers were getting stuck into the grog. Suddenly, one of them tumbled off his bar stool and rolled across the floor and lay there without moving a muscle or a hair on his head.

'One thing about Bill,' his drinking mate offered to the worried barman, 'he knows when to stop.'

THE APPLE ISLE

This boozer was holding court in the bar and going on and on about Tasmanians.

'They're either footballers or bloody prostitutes,' he said.

A big, burly bloke came nearer to the boozer and drew himself up to his full height of six foot eight.

'Listen mate, I want you to know that my wife is a Tasmanian.'

Before he could utter another word, the loudmouth looked at him, very interested and cool.

'Really? What team does she play for?'

THE PRESERVATION OF THE AUSSIE MALE

The horse and mule live thirty years
And nothing know of wine and beers.
The goat and sheep at twenty die
With never a taste of scotch or rye.
The cow drinks water by the ton
And at eighteen years is mostly done.
The dog at sixteen cashes in
Without the aid of rum or gin.
The cat in milk and water soaks
And then in twelve short years it croaks.

The modest, sober, bone-dry hen
Lays eggs for nogs and dies at ten.
All animals are strictly dry
They sinless live and quickly die.
But sinful, gin-full, rum-soaked men
Survive for three score years and ten.
And some of us, the mighty few
Stay pickled till we're ninety-two.

EIGHTEEN BOTTLES OF WHISKY

The old bushie had eighteen bottles of whisky in his cellar and, after a particularly rowdy night, his long-suffering wife insisted he pour every single bottle down the sink or she would leave him. That afternoon, he stood in the pub and told his mates of the horrible experience.

'Reluctantly, I started on my unpleasant task as I withdrew the first cork and commenced pouring the whisky down the sink. I couldn't help myself from drinking a glass first. I withdrew the cork from the second bottle and did likewise with it and scoffed yet another glass. I withdrew the cork from the third bottle and poured the contents down the sink, which I drank. I pulled the cork from the fourth and drank the sink out of it, then threw the bottle down the glass. I pulled the sink out of the next glass and poured the cork down the bottle. Then I corked the sink with the glass, bottled the drink and drank the house. Then, when I had everything emptied, I steadied the house with the one hand, counted the glasses, corks, bottles and sinks (which came to twenty-nine) and, as the house came by again, I counted them all again and finally had all the houses in the one bottle which I then drank.'

The old timer looked at the puzzled assembly and added: 'I am not under the ofluence of incohol as some thinkle peep I am. I am not half as thunk as you drink I am. I don't know who is me and the drunker I stand the longer I get!?'

THE DRINKER'S DREAM

Do you remember the summer of '63
That melted the rocks of the back country?
The year the sand fused into glass,
And the sun burnt the gorge in Murchison Pass?

Well, I was there in that terrible heat,
Where borders of West and South Australia meet,
About 900 miles from Oonapelli.
That was the time I met Ned Kelly.

Out of the simmering, heat-haze fog,
Strode Kelly, with arms loaded with grog,
'I'm Kelly, alright!' he said to me,
'And I'm twice as dead as you'll ever be.'

'For ninety years I wandered this place,
In search of a suitable drinking mate.'
'You've found him!' I quickly said,
'So let's put some of these bottles to bed.'

We drank in the sun and talked of days
When men wore guts where they now wear stays.
Then came the thump of many feet,
As heavy boots thudded through that stifling heat.

A line of men fractured the desert haze,
'Twas old Paddy Hannan — Gawd spare me days!
Followed by Thunderbolt, Burke and Wills,
Ben Hall, Captain Moonlight and Saltbush Bill.

Each carried some grog — cold as a tomb —
So Ned and I moved, gave them some room,
To place the keg that was carried by Hall,
Fair in the centre, and on tap to all.

Then in strode Lawson and Ludwig Leichhardt,
Who said: 'Lassiter's coming, but it's okay to start,
I've invited some friends from the desert nearby,
And they're all decent blokes, here's dust in your eye!'

We were joined by a bright green kangaroo,
And an overweight wombat, who did a soft shoe,
A dignified dingo, with performing fleas,
And a soprano galah who squawked off-key.

And a sabre-toothed snake whistled: 'Old Lang Syne',
While a marsupial mouse, with his nose, twitched time.
We sat in the sun and we drank for a week,
In the finest company a man could keep.

I danced me a jig, for comic relief,
And in disturbing the dust found Lassiter's Reef.
There was copper and nickel and silver galore,
Diamonds the size of a knob on a door.

Rubies and sapphires — a fabulous haul —
And ten pounds of gold to each shovel full.
But none gave a thought to such meaningless wealth,
For each was contented unto himself.

After we'd drank for a year and a day,
The party broke up and we went our own ways.
I travelled south to the Nullarbor Plains,
And in two or three days was back home again.

But I said not a word of where I had been,
And never recounted the things I had seen.
But the experience taught me one important fact:
Never drink in the sun without wearing a hat!

A DROP OF BEER

I was up in far north Queensland and having a quiet drink when into the hotel bar comes this grizzled old swaggie with a face that looked as dry as the One Tree Plain.

He sauntered up to the bar, looked at me and says: 'Could you spare a traveller a drop of beer?'

Now, I didn't have a lot of cash, so I handed him the schooner of beer I had just started on and he ups it and, strike me blue, he drinks the bloody lot!

'I thought you said that you only wanted a drop!'

For a reply, he took a long look at me and said: 'Yes, my friend, I only wanted a drop but it was that drop at the very bottom of the glass.'

With that he thanked me and departed.

BOTTLES GETS A JOB

Old 'Bottles' Bentley had a hatred of work. They used to joke that he wouldn't work in an iron lung. On top of that, Bottles had a fondness for the drink and would more often than not end up in the local police station charged with drunk and disorderly behaviour. The local circuit magistrate had seen him so many times that his patience was wearing thin with making threats.

'Mr Bentley, you have become an unwelcome visitor to these Chambers. If I see you again, you will leave me no option but gaol. I will give you one final chance and I want your word that you will get a steady job and settle down.'

Bottles looked at the magistrate and swore he'd be a reformed man and get a job. Three days later, there was Bottles Bentley back in court on the same old charge.

'Weren't you going to get a job and stop this nonsense?' asked the magistrate.

'I did, yer Worship. I had a good job as a ringbarker.'

The weary magistrate looked at him suspiciously and asked: 'Oh really? Where?'

'On the One-Tree Plain, yer Worship,' was the response.

BLUEY BRINK

There once was a shearer by name Bluey Brink,
A devil for work and a terror for drink,
He could shear his two hundred a day without fear,
And drink without winking, four gallons of beer.

Now Jimmy the barman, who served out the drink,
He hated the sight of this here Bluey Brink,
Who stayed much too late and who came much too soon,
At morning, at evening, at night and at noon.

One morning, as Jimmy was cleaning the bar
With sulphuric acid he kept in a jar,
Old Bluey came yelling and bawling with thirst,
'Whatever you got, Jim, just hand me that first!'

Now, it ain't put in history, it ain't down in print,
But Bluey drank acid with never a wink,
Saying: 'That's the stuff, Jimmy, why, strike me stone dead,
This'll make me the ringer of Stephenson's shed.'

Now all the next day as he served out the beer,
Poor Jimmy was sick with his trouble and fear,
Too worried to argue, too anxious to fight,
Seeing that shearer a corpse in the night.

But early next morning, as he opened the door,
Along came old Bluey, howling for more,
With his eyebrows all singed and his whiskers deranged,
And holes in his hide like a dog with the mange.

Says Jimmy: 'And how did you like the new stuff?'
Says Bluey: 'It's fine, but I ain't had enough;
It gives me great courage to shear and to fight,
But why does that stuff set my whiskers alight?

I thought I knew drink, but I must have been wrong,
For what you just gave me was proper and strong,
It set me to coughing, and you know I'm no liar,
And every damn cough set me whiskers on fire!'

(Traditional song)

DIVE IN, THE WATER'S FINE

Two swaggies had been on a terrible drinking spree and were walking out of town in an attempt to sober up.

'Look at that, will you?' cried one as he pointed to a waving field of wheat. 'I think I'll dive in and have a swim in that beautiful water.'

He dived into the wheat and immediately resurfaced holding his fractured skull.

'Ouch! Don't try it. The bottom's on the bloody top.'

> *I'm getting over the worst hangover*
> *That I've ever had before.*
> *The first was a whisky,*
> *The second was gin,*
> *The third was a beer with a cigarette in.*
> *There's no use explaining the one remaining —*
> *It's all over the kitchen floor.*
> *I'm getting over the worst hangover*
> *That I've ever had before.*
>
> **(Traditional parody)**

WHEN O'DOOLEY DRINKS, EVERYONE DRINKS!

Weather-strained, and blinking from the dust of a 100-mile ride, the old prospector pushed his way through the door of the crowded goldfields pub where he faced the publican.

'Drinks are on me!' he shouted. 'When O'Dooley drinks, everybody drinks.'

To the publican he said: 'And 'ave one yerself.'

Glasses filled to the brim, the miners turned to salute and congratulate the old prospector.

Presently the smiling publican presented the account. 'Fifteen quid, old chap.'

'Sorry, I haven't had much luck of late, can't pay yer,' was the astonishing response.

The publican, his face flaming red with anger, leapt over the bar, clouted the old bloke, and tossed him out of the door into the street.

Business had resumed in the hotel and ten minutes later, the old prospector pushed his way through the crowd and made his way towards the bar again.

'Drinks are on me!' he shouted. 'When O'Dooley drinks, everyone drinks.'

The publican, looking as if he was about to have an apoplectic fit, made a violent turn towards the old man.

The prospector fiercely wagged his finger at the approaching publican. 'And you're not 'aving one this time. You can't hold yer grog!'

COULDN'T WALK IN THEM!

The old swag-carrier was dying for a drink and entered the hotel carrying a pair of boots.

'I say, old man, I'm afraid I have accidentally run out of cash and I was wondering if you'd accept these excellent riding boots in exchange for a couple of schooners.'

The barman, impressed with the swagman's polite approach, and figuring that he could do with a new pair of riding boots, agreed to the offer.

As the swaggie quickly knocked off the two schooners, the barman held up the boots, which were falling to pieces and full of holes, saying: 'Struth, mate, these are the worst pair of boots I've ever seen. What makes you think they're riding boots?'

'Well,' observed the old sage, 'yer couldn't walk in 'em.'

SATAN!

Mrs O'Toole had about enough of her husband's drinking sprees and decided to try and scare him out of his habit. One Friday night, she hid herself behind a thick bush and waited for him to roll his way home from the rubbity-dub. When he came along the track she jumped out in front of him.

'Struth! Who the hell are you?' he cried.

'Satan!' came the deep, disguised reply.

Bill O'Toole's hand shot out like an arrow. 'Shake hands, you old son of a gun! I married yer sister!'

DEAD-END DRINKERS

Two old-timers had been drinking at the same hotel bar on the same day, at the same hour, every week for nigh on fifteen years. One day, only one of the men arrived.

'Where's your mate?' asked the barman with obvious surprise.

'He got burned,' replied the old fellow with a forlorn shake of his noggin.

'Cheer up,' said the barman, 'he'll be up and around again soon.'

'Don't know about that,' answered the lonely one, glumly. 'I don't think they mess about down at that there crematorium.'

DROVERS
ON THE OUTSIDE
TRACK

Have you ever been droving out west?
Where the flies are a terrible pest,
And the mosquitoes at night, by Jesus they bite,
And the bulldog ants in your blankets at night,
By the Jesus you know you're earning your dough,
When you take on droving out west.
(**Traditional poem**)

The life of the drover was one of endless riding as cattle were pushed across the country and fattened for the market. It was a lonely life, and one where songs and yarn-telling were an important way for the men to retain their sanity. Sometimes, the drover's dog was the only audience — a very grateful one at that. Like the shearers, the drovers were seen as mighty, almost superhuman men, and stories about them tend to be exaggerated in true tall-tale tradition.

A GOOD PIG

A drover walked into a country pub with a three-legged pig on a leash. The barmaid looked at the drover and then at the pig.

'Two beers, please,' ordered the drover. 'One for me and one for my pig.'

The barmaid was still staring at the pig as she took the order and offered: 'Must be some pig.'

The drover looked at the pig proudly and said: 'This pig is one in a million and he goes wherever I go.'

'What makes him so special?' enquired the barmaid.

'He saved my son from drowning in the dam, just waded in and dragged the little lad out. Yes, some special pig alright.'

The drover noticed that the pig had finished his beer, so he ordered another two schooners.

'Yes,' the drover continued, 'then not long after saving my son's life, our house caught fire and the pig raised the alarm and dragged us all clear. Darn well saved the whole family from being burnt to a crisp. Yes, some special pig alright.'

The barmaid placed the beers on the counter and looked down at the pig. 'Is that how he lost his leg?'

'Nah!' said the drover as he downed his beer. 'A pig that special — you can't eat him all at once!'

WHICH ROUTE?

Queensland's best-known stockman, Billy Dale, had decided to make the big trip to Sydney and all his mates had gathered in the pub for the send off. There was much singing and bragging and, eventually, some toasts.

'Hey, Billy! You're off to the big smoke — are you sure you know the way? Tell us which route ya gonna take?'

At this, Billy took the stage and explained: 'I've decided to take the missus, after all, she stuck with me right through the Depression!'

A BAD HORSE

A Texan rancher was visiting the Northern Territory, inspecting cattle stations. Everything was always bigger and better back home in Texas. As he was being shown around a particularly big station he asked: 'Now, just how big is this here ranch?'

The station owner nodded and said: 'Well, about 1000 square miles and if I get on my horse I can be at the boundary in a few hours.'

The Texan nodded, adding: 'Well, my ranch is so big that I can get on my horse and ride the darn thing all day and by sunset I still won't have reached the boundary fence.'

The Australian glanced once at the Texan and said: 'Yeah, mate, I used to have a horse like that.'

DIDN'T GO THAT WAY

Bill the drover was boasting to his mates about his great droving exploits.

'Yes, I've drove cattle, sheep and even fowls.'

He had been chewing the fat for over an hour and the men were getting tired of his jaw breaking. One man looked up and put his hand out for silence.

'Listen, Bill, you might be a decent drover but you're not a patch on me. I once had the hardest droving job in livin' history! I had to take a mob of 2000 Murray cod from Albury to the Atherton Tablelands and I didn't lose one scale!'

The men cheered until a wiry old fellow at the back of the bar moved in.

'Argh, you new chums! You want to know about real drovin' listen t'me. I once had a job to drove 5000 barrels of Bundaberg rum from Queensland to Hobart. We gave them a push start, they rolled on down across the New South Wales border, down through the Snowy Mountains, past Melbourne and eventually we landed in Hobart Town. Only lost one wayward barrel!'

Bill gave the newcomer a hard look and said: 'Well, friend, what the hell did you do about Bass Strait?'

'Oh, we didn't go that way,' replied the old-timer.

COLD CHOPS

A couple of hard-bitten bushmen were discussing how really bitterly cold it could get in the Victorian Ranges.

'I remember,' offered Mulga Dan, 'when I wuz droving sheep up near Mount Buffalo. The sheep in the lead came to a deep ditch in the snow and just stopped at the edge. He stood there and the sheep behind him jumped over his back and, you wouldn't read about it, he just stuck there in the air, frozen solid. Then another sheep jumped over him and he also froze as hard as a brick, then another and another until they had formed a sort of sheep bridge for the others to run over. It was an incredible sight.'

Old Bert had been around the block a few times himself, and wasn't going to take this yarn without a challenge.

'Arr, Dan, that's bloody impossible. The force of gravity just wouldn't allow it.'

'Well, that's all you bloody well know,' drawled Mulga Dan, 'that was frozen too.'

BAD AIM

Two drovers were camped by the road for the night. After their meal they sat around the fire talking and, eventually, one of them got up and wandered over to the fence for a leak. After a minute or so he yelled out to his mate: 'Hey, Col, you ever smoked a cigarette that's been pissed on?'

The other drover thought this over for a few minutes and replied: 'Nar, I can't say that I have.'

More silence followed and then: 'Can't say that you've missed much.'

THE BILLYGOAT OVERLAND

Come all you lads of the droving days, ye gentlemen unafraid,
I'll tell you about the strangest trip that ever a drover made,
For we rolled our swags and packed our bags, and taking our lives in hand,
We started away with a thousand goats on the Billygoat Overland.

There wasn't a fence that'd hold the mob, to keep them from their desires,
They skipped along the top of the posts and cake-walked on the wire,
And whenever the lanes were bare of grass and the paddocks were nice and green,
Oh, the goats they travelled outside the lanes, and we rode in between!

The squatters started to drive them back, but that was no good at all!
The horses ran for the lick of their lives from scent that was like a wall,
And never a dog had pluck enough in front of the mob to stand
And face the charge of a thousand goats on the Billygoat Overland.

We found we were hundreds over strength when we started to count the mob,
And they put us in gaol for a crowd of thieves that travelled to steal and rob,
For every goat between here and Bourke that scented this spicy band,
Had left his home and friends to join the Billygoat Overland.

(A.B. 'Banjo' Paterson)

STUFF ME!

Two drovers were working as a team and taking a mob of fat cattle down from Nyngan to Wagga Wagga. Like most drovers they were quiet sort of fellows, content enough to share a few words over a cuppa and that was about enough talk for a day. Passing through a small town, one of them spotted a sign for the local taxidermist and, as he pushed his mob along the feed tracks, he couldn't help but wonder what the hell a taxidermist was.

That night, around the campfire, he nodded to his mate and said: 'Bert, did you happen to see the sign for the taxidermist in the town?'

Bert gave a thoughtful grunt and, with a sigh, replied. 'As a matter of fact, I did see that sign but I ain't got a clue what it means.'

'Got me bushed, too,' Bill said.

A week or so later, they hit Wagga Wagga.

As they shook hands and said goodbye, Bill added: 'I found out about that taxidermist bloke — he stuffs cows, dogs, sheep and horses.'

'Oh blimey, he's a drover, eh.'

SANDY
THE SHEARER

Sandy is a mythical shearer of Australia. He is a Scot and true to the canny tradition of the kilt-wearers.

He appears to get around quite a bit and there are stories about how he lived in Sydney, travelled to various international destinations and we also get to hear about some of his private life. Like all good folklore characters, we can recognise familiar faces in the yarns.

SANDY ON HOLIDAY

Sandy had decided to take his wife on a holiday.

Halfway to New Zealand, his wife started to continually nag and complain. 'Sandy, for heaven's sake, I don't want to go on holidays. I don't want to go to New Zealand!'

Sandy shot her a harsh look. 'Don't be silly, you're nearly there — keep swimming!'

SANDY'S WIFE'S FALSE TEETH

Two Scotchmen were catching up and exchanging small talk.

'How yer been keeping, Sandy?'

'Well, Col, to tell you the truth, not too good. I lost me health and had to give the job away, I'm poor as a church mouse and then me teeth went crook — I had to get a pair of them false teeth. Nar, I haven't been too good.'

He then started to cough and splutter and reached for his handkerchief, and as he unfolded it a pair of false teeth fell out.

'What on earth possessed a canny man like yourself to buy two pairs of teeth, Sandy?'

'Oh, this pair isn'a mine — they belong to the wife. I carry them with me so she doesn't eat between meals!'

MEAT BILL

The butcher, who was worried about collecting a large, overdue account, approached Sandy cautiously.

'Before you order anything else, I think I should let you know your bill is a lot larger than it should be.'

'Aye,' nodded Sandy. 'Now we're getting somewhere! Tell me what you think it should be and I'll settle up.'

SANDY'S LUNCH

Sandy came back to his boarding house after work, only to be met by the landlady who looked extremely worried.

'Sandy, did you eat those sandwiches I made for you for lunch today?'

'Yes, of course I ate them,' said Sandy.

'Did you enjoy them, Sandy?' she asked.

'Yeah, they were fine,' replied Sandy. 'Why? What was wrong with them?'

'Oh nothing,' said the canny landlady. 'It's just that you'll have to polish your brown shoes with fish paste tomorrow.'

SANDY IN VENICE

Sandy had spent a lifetime as a drover and he had always dreamed of travelling to Italy to see the magic of Venice. By sheer fortune, he won a QANTAS competition in the *Land* newspaper — the prize was a trip to Europe, so Sandy went to Venice. On his return, his mates met in the pub and they all wanted to hear about Venice. Sandy didn't appear to be too generous with his appreciation of the great city.

'I guess it was alright, but just my bloody luck to visit when all the bloody roads were flooded!'

ART LOVER

When Sandy was planning his overseas holiday, one of the local wealthy squatters asked him whether he would do a favour for him and purchase either a Van Gogh or a Cézanne. Sandy thought about it, and refused on the grounds that our economy needed all the help it could get.

'Those small European cars are okay,' he lectured, 'but you should really buy an Australian-made Ford or Holden.'

SANDY IN LONDON

Sandy won the lotto and decided to take a trip to Scotland and then to London. He also decided that his daughter would take the trip with him. There they were riding around in an open-topped London Explorer Bus when it started to spit with a light rain.

Sandy, ever protective of his daughter, called downstairs: 'Is there a mackintosh to keep my daughter warm?'

The response came back immediately: 'No, but there's a McKenzie that'll give her a go!'

SANDY IN SYDNEY

One year, Sandy decided to give the droving season a miss and try his luck in Sydney. As luck would have it, he landed a job immediately with the lads who kept the horses at Randwick Racecourse. He also got some accommodation at a boarding house in nearby Darlinghurst. The deal was twenty-five pounds a week, which included a cut lunch. On his first day, he was met at the front door by the boarding house lady, who handed him a tomato and cheese sandwich for his lunch.

'Here's your lunch, Sandy. Enjoy it!'

Off he went and when he returned at 5 o'clock, the landlady met him at the door.

'How did you enjoy your lunch, Sandy?'

'It was very good but there was'na enough,' he replied.

She didn't say anything and the next morning she went into the kitchen and made him two big sandwiches of cheese and tomato. Handing them to him, she bid him goodbye and said: 'Enjoy your lunch, Sandy.'

When he arrived home, she met him at the front door and enquired: 'Did you enjoy your lunch, Sandy?'

'It was bonny, missus, but there was'na enough.'

She didn't say anything, and next morning she took a whole tank loaf and cut it down the middle and proceeded to layer it up with cheese and tomato. It was a whopper! As he left, she repeated: 'Enjoy your lunch, Sandy.'

On his return that evening, she once again met him at the door and asked the usual question. 'Did you enjoy your lunch, Sandy?'

'Aye, missus, 'twas very nice but I see you're back to the one sandwich again!'

SANDY'S SPONGE CAKE

Farmer Sandy was always proud of his wife's ability to make a meal out of practically nothing.

'What are we having for afternoon tea?' he asked one fine day.

'Sponge cake, dear,' said Sandy's proud wife. 'I sponged the eggs off Mrs Doughty, the flour off Mrs O'Toole and the milk off Mrs O'Malley.'

SANDY'S NEW ROOM

Sandy was after a new boarding house, and the cheerful landlady was making a fuss to show him her various rooms. They climbed several stairs and she ushered him into a small, dingy room.

'Well, what do you think of it as a whole?' she enquired.

'Oh,' said Sandy. 'I guess it's alright for a hole, but I was really after a bedroom.'

SANDY GOES TO THE FLICKS

Sandy went to the picture theatre and started to interrogate the young box office lass about the film.

'Is it worth ten shillings a ticket?' he questioned.

He kept on her case and started to question her about the script.

'It's about a doctor,' replied the young girl helpfully.

'A doctor!' Sandy exclaimed. 'If you're going to charge me ten shillings to see a film about a doctor, tell me this: is he a specialist?'

A BARGAIN PRICE

Sandy, always counting his money, was offered some lambs at five shillings each.

'Five bob a lamb!' he exclaimed with shock. 'That's a wee bit steep!'

The local stock agent looked him straight in the eye and said: 'Alright, Sandy, you can have them for three quid a dozen.'

'That's more bloody like it, I'll have them.'

WHISKY

Many years ago, when whisky was ten shillings and sixpence, old McTavish went down to his local to buy his usual Friday night bottle. After searching his pockets, he discovered he was a shilling short. He knew well the publican's strict policy of 'no credit to anyone under any circumstance', so McTavish raced out into the street and spotted Sandy walking his dog.

'Sandy, my man, can you do me a favour and lend me a shilling?'

'What for, McTavish?'

'To buy a bottle of whisky.'

Sandy swiftly dipped his hand into his pocket and said to McTavish: 'Here's two shillings — buy one for me too.'

SANDY IN HAWAII

Sandy won a trip to Hawaii. He was very excited about spending time on the glorious beaches and even had a fantasy about meeting some nice young girls. He had been there two days and not one girl had even looked at him, let alone spoken to him. He was in the bar that night, and got to talking to the barman.

'How do you attract girls on the beach, mate?' he asked.

'It all depends, my friend, but I have a sure-fire trick that really gets them chasing you.'

Sandy was all ears. He really would like to tell his mates back home about the girls. 'Please, tell me your secret?' he asked the barman.

'Well, I'll tell you what to do. Get a large potato and stick it down your swimming costume. You'll have the girls chasing you all right.'

So that's exactly what Sandy did. He paraded up and down the beach all day, strutted like a peacock, and the girls were looking and giggling. He wasn't sure how long he was supposed to walk with the potato in his swimwear but decided to do it for the full day.

That evening he sat, looking very dejected, at the bar.

'How did you go, my man?' enquired the barman.

'Bloody hopeless,' was Sandy's reply. 'I did exactly what you told me, and the girls looked but when I went up to them, they screamed and ran away.'

'They did?' It was then the barman realised what the problem had been.

'Sandy, my man, you're supposed to put the potato down the front of your swimming trunks!'

BUSH
ROMANCE

Here's to the tree of life,
Long may it stand.
It grows upon two rocks,
Upon the Isle of Man.
Here's to that little plant,
That doth around it twine.
It comes in flower every month,
And bears fruit once in nine.

(**Traditional toast**)

It is true that early Australia, and especially the outback, was a male-dominated world. Some would say that the bush was no place for a woman, but that is simply not true. It came down to the fact that the majority of work was hard yakka that demanded muscle. The men also lived in very close quarters in sub-standard conditions. There's a line in one of our most popular bush songs, 'The Banks of the Condamine', where the departing shearer replies to his girl's plea to allow her to join him.

Although we do have a body of traditional love songs, the yarns tend to be more rough and ready. Fairly sexist stuff but typical of the era and, after all, it's all fairly naïve and awkward as they show the gawky bushman and his efforts to make love.

Oh Nancy, dearest Nancy, with me you cannot go,
The squatters have given orders, love, no woman should do so.
Your delicate constitution is not equal unto mine,
To stand the constant tigering on the banks of the Condamine.

(**Traditional song**)

SEE THE COOK

A fellow got a job out west and after lasting for several months without the company of a woman, he asked the head stockman what they did about sex.

'Well,' said the stockman, 'if you're really desperate you can go and see the cook, but it will cost you sixty quid.'

'Sixty flamin' quid!' he exclaimed. 'The bastard must be getting bloody rich at that rate.'

'Ah, well, not exactly,' said the stockman. 'Look, it's like this: you have to sling the manager twenty quid, because he doesn't approve of that sort of thing.

'And you have to slip the foreman twenty quid, because he doesn't approve of that sort of thing.

'And then, of course, you have to pay two of the blokes ten quid each to hold the cook — he doesn't approve of that sort of thing either!'

MAN'S BEST FRIEND

The grizzled old-timer lived out the back of Woop Woop, and one of his few delights was showing off his prize possession — an old, single-barrelled shotgun.

'It's not much to look at,' he would eagerly confide to his fellow drinkers, 'and it'll never be written up in any of those history books, but this here gun of mine has got every one of my four daughters married off good and proper.'

THAT'S ONE!

The old farmer didn't say too much. The locals said that he had hardly muttered 200 words in all the years they had known him.

They also reckoned that his wife said enough for the both of them. She never seemed to shut her mouth!

One morning, they were headed to town in the old wagonette and, for some reason or other the old horse Dobbin had taken it to mind to keep stopping to feed on the grass which lined the road. The farmer was becoming very annoyed, and every time the horse refused to shift, he would sit there, ready to explode.

The next time the horse stopped, the farmer jumped from the wagon and stood in front of the horse and yelled out: 'That's one!'

After a couple of miles, Dobbin decided that it was rest time again — and so he did. Once again, the infuriated farmer jumped from the wagon, faced the horse and yelled: 'That's two!'

Another few miles had passed when the horse stopped yet again. This time, the farmer jumped from the wagon and yelled: 'That's three!' and with that, he shot the horse stone dead!

All the while the wife had not shut her mouth once — complaining about him, the horse, the gun, the heat and anything else she could think of. This final episode only made her tongue go twice as fast.

The farmer eyeballed his wife and shouted: 'That's one!'

They say the wife shut up after that!

HELP!

The old prospector had struck it rich, and his wife decided they should quit the bush and buy a waterfront house in Surfers Paradise. The prospector was reluctant — he liked his old ways — however, his wife would not give in and was very excited about moving up in society. She arranged for them to attend the opera, the ballet, art gallery openings and anything else that opens, but she could never stop his rowdy ways.

One day they decided to go swimming and she heard a man shout: 'Help! Help! I'm drowning!' She wandered down to the water's edge. To her horror, it was her husband, so she started back again.

'Please, George, not so loud!'

BOSTON STRANGLER

It was lunch time at the abattoir and Bert was explaining to the men how his wife had ear-bashed him last night for having sexist attitudes. This puzzled the men, and none of them could explain what sexism actually was. Bert decided to ask the manager if he could give them an example of sexism.

'Well,' the manager said, 'supposing some ugly-looking bloke knocks at your door and tells you that he's the Boston Strangler, it would be very sexist if you then yelled out to your wife: "Darling, it's for you!"'

TRAINING A DINGO

A drover once trapped a young dingo and decided to try and raise it to be a working dog. Try as he might, the dingo would not settle down, so the drover decided to place an advertisement in the *Land* newspaper seeking someone who could train a wild dog. He received two applications — one from a young, attractive blonde, and the other from a weather-beaten rabbiter who looked like he'd seen a few years in the scrub.

The pretty girl was the first to use her skills to try to tame the dingo. She entered the cage and commenced talking to the wild dog in a smooth, quiet voice, calling it 'sweetie' and 'darling'. The dog responded by walking over to the girl and nuzzling its head between her bare legs as she continued patting it gently.

The dog's owner was astonished at how placid the beast had become. He turned to the rabbiter and asked: 'Can you do that?'

'You bet your life I can!' replied the rabbiter, enthusiastically. 'If you can get that bloody dingo out of there!'

DAD'S PERMISSION

The young shearer bolted into the church, holding his shears in one hand and his girlfriend in the other. He was sweating like a pig and could hardly be understood, he was babbling so much.

'Help!' he managed to scream. 'We want to get married right now.'

The priest attempted to be priestly and serene but the young man would have none of that.

'We want a marriage ceremony right now!' he blurted out.

The priest said: 'Now, there are certain obligations and routines associated with the holy ceremony of marriage.'

The shearer was becoming increasingly frustrated and belted out: 'Be blowed with your rules — we want to be married right now!'

'For one thing,' continued the priest, 'you must have consent from the young girl's father.'

'Be blowed!' bellowed the young man, gesturing towards the window. 'See that old bloke out there with the shotgun? That's her father and he consents!'

PULL THE OTHER LEG

Australians have a saying: 'Pull the other leg, it's got bells on it!', implying derision, scorn and disbelief of what has been said. This doesn't prevent us from being the biggest tellers of whoppers in the entire world, and where there's an audience, preferably with drink in hand, then those lies will be sure to flow as yarn-tellers compete with one another to produce the most unlikely stories which, of course, they fully expect the audience to believe.

THE WATTLE FLAT RAM

There was a young ram from Wattle Flat,
Who had three horns of brass.
Two grew out of his forehead, sir,
The other grew out of his . . .

Inki dinki darby
Inki dinki day
He was the finest ram, sir,
That ever fed on hay.

This ram was mighty frisky,
He lived on the best of grass.
And any ewe from thereabouts,
Got a burst right up the . . .

When this ram was in his prime,
They showed him off in a truck.
And all the ewes from roundabout,
They came round for a . . .

When this ram grew older,
He grew a fleece so thick,
It took ten men and a rouseabout,
To find the head of his . . .

When this ram was shorn,
They got an awful shock.
He had eighteen inches of wool, sir,
And only one inch of . . .

When the ram died,
They took him to St Paul's.
It took eight men and a rouseabout,
To carry one of his . . .

If you don't believe me,
Take it as a lie.
But anybody from Wattle Flat,
Will tell you the same as I.

PUMPKIN PICKING

In the outback of Australia, it is not that unusual to find giant vegetables growing — especially after the rainy season.

Several years ago, I heard about a farmer up near Brewarrina who told his son to go and chop a big piece — 'enough to fill a four-horse wagon' — off their giant pumpkin to take to market. I observed that it must have been a very big pumpkin if a slice would fill a wagon! He assured me it was.

Apparently, the farmer helped his son by holding the ladder steady as the lad climbed inside the pumpkin to chop the slice. He'd lost sight of him but heard the reassuring chop, chop, chop of the axe. After a couple of hours, the lad still hadn't returned, so the farmer shouted a cooee or two but there was no response. He decided he would have to venture inside and look for the boy. He walked a mile or so inside the pumpkin, but there was no sight of his son, although he did come across a bullock driver who had the audacity to ask him what he was doing in the pumpkin! Apparently, the bullocky had his own problems — he'd lost his team a week ago and was still looking for it! He said he'd say hello to the farmer's son if he saw him!

A LITTLE BULL

Early in the morning, three bulls set off on the road together — a hefty Hereford, a stalwart Shorthorn and a little runt of a Jersey bull. The plan was to walk to greener pastures, but they had hardly travelled any distance when they came to a beautiful paddock with luscious grass, clear running water and several nice-looking heifers.

'Look boys,' said the Hereford, 'this looks alright to me — I can live like a king here.' He jumped the fence, scared off the resident bull, and wandered off to inspect his domain.

The two remaining bulls continued their journey along the dusty roads and, by and by, they came across another fine-looking paddock, which the Shorthorn declared was 'as good as the finest he had ever seen', and here, too, was water, feed and heifers. He jumped the fence, evicted the resident bull and inspected his new home.

The little bull continued on his travels — he passed paddock after paddock, all desirable but all with a threatening resident bull. Onwards and onwards he was forced to travel and he could possibly still be travelling, which goes to prove the old adage: a little bull goes a long way!

THE HAT

The two timber cutters were headed to Sydney after the wet season had put a damper on their work. As they rode along the track, they spotted an old Akubra hat on the side of the road.

'Hey! Isn't that Prickly Pete's hat?' one asked.

'I'll go and take a look,' said the other.

When they picked up the hat they found Pete's head under it and he was up to his ears in mud.

'Help me out of here, fellers.'

They got him out but he said he was a little worried about his team. Apparently, he had been standing on the wagon — they were in pretty deep!

THE GOANNA ON THE PIANO

In the old days, travelling showmen often arrived in a town and hired the town hall or the school of arts hall, and then they would set about promoting their show. One day, a rickety old sulky arrived in town carrying an even more run-down old-timer who claimed to be Australia's oldest and most successful showman. He trotted off to the local school of arts hall and commenced negotiating with the manager, a stubborn type of fellow known locally as 'Doubting Thomas'.

The old bloke started his spiel: 'I have a show that will fill this hall for a week, however, I'm a bit low in the pocket at this point so I'd be looking at half the usual rental fee.'

The hall manager's reply was short and not so sweet as he declared: 'No bloody way!'

The haggling went back and forth until the showman, getting rather exasperated, confided in a hushed breath: 'Look, my good man, I will make a deal with you but you must keep it under your hat. How about you give me the use of this hall for free and I will share the profits with you?'

This seemed to stir some sort of entrepreneurial interest in Doubting Thomas, whose only comment was: 'Continue. What exactly is this act? Dancing girls? Country yodellers?'

The old showman's voice dropped to a barely audible whisper, and with the manager's ear stuck close to his mouth he explained: 'This is the most extraordinary show of the modern age. I've a goanna that plays the piano and a carpet snake that has a voice like Peter Dawson.'

Doubting Thomas's eyes popped out in fury, and he was tempted to boff the old man but thought better of it. He was just about to boot the geezer out the door when the showman reached down and picked up his brown hessian bag, and out of it he took a huge goanna.

'Where's the piano?' he demanded.

The showman placed the goanna on the piano stool, with claws ready on the keyboard, and then he dove into the bag and bought out an extremely well-fed carpet snake, which he placed on the piano top.

'Okay fellers, strike up the music!'

And they did just that, launching right into 'I'll Linger Longer in Yarrawonga', which the goanna played in old stride style with the snake crooning along. It was a fabulous act and Doubting Thomas could see the potential — they'd come from far and wide!

'You've got a deal!' he shouted. 'And I want exclusive rights to Queensland and New South Wales!'

The old-timer simply looked at the manager and picked up his hessian bag, placed the snake back into the bag and then he did the same with the goanna. 'Sorry, I've changed my mind, too many restrictions.'

The manager was becoming quite hysterical, screaming at the old boy, offering all manner of financial gain. As this didn't seem to work, he decided on another approach and found himself on his knees begging the old man to explain his change of heart.

'Well,' confided the old man, 'you have a terrible reputation with my fellow showies and I wanted to see just how bad you really were. And besides, I am a truthful man and not deceitful and since my show is based on illusion, I didn't want to trick you.'

Now this really confused Doubting Thomas — he didn't know which way to turn.

'What the hell are you talking about?' he screamed. 'I saw the act myself!'

'Well,' said the showman, 'to tell you the honest truth, the snake is an ordinary carpet snake and it can't sing at all — that there goanna is a ventriloquist!'

BIG BIRDS IN THE BUSH

The new chum was travelling up-country for the first time and was full of questions about the outback and the native bird life in particular.

'And what is the smallest bird in the Australian bush?' he enquired.

'That would be our tiny tom-tits,' replied the station ringer.

'And what would be the largest bird?'

'Arh, that would be the emu — the largest bird in the entire world,' sighed the ringer.

Time passed and they were driving through a small town and the new chum excitedly pointed to the local schoolyard where they had two tame emus pecking their way around the playground.

'Look! Look! What are those birds?'

The driver glanced over and laconically mumbled: 'Those? They're tom-tits, mate.'

CROOKED MICK OF THE SPEEWAH

The indigenous people of Australia have many epic stories which belong to their 'Dreaming', however, the European settlers have no such tradition, so they had to invent one. We did not transplant the British and Celtic stories concerning dragon-slaying knights, mischievous fairy folk and milkmaids being rolled in the newly mown hay. We had no war heroes or age-old mythology, so we made heroes out of our workers and sportsmen. Crooked Mick of the Speewah is the best-known cultural hero representing our rural past. He appears to have first surfaced in print in the 1920s when a shearer's union worker named Julian Stuart recalled yarns in circulation during the 1880s. In the interest of the tradition, I have reworked several old and recent tales about this extraordinary man and the place where he was born.

THE SPEEWAH

Australia is a strange country with an outback that covers most of the country. It's bigger than anything you could ever imagine and that includes Texas — we've got cattle stations bigger than Texas! One of the strangest places in the outback is the famed Speewah, home to Crooked Mick.

The Speewah is a big place out near the Never-Never, way past the legendary Black Stump, past the town of Woop Woop and somewhere between Gulargambone and Mooloogooloo. It's way past the backblocks, in the land where the crows fly backwards (to keep the dust out of their eyes). You can't miss it!

The strangest thing about the Speewah is its climate. It can be so swelteringly hot one side of the barbed wire rabbit-proof fence that drovers need to wear an asbestos suit, and so bloody cold on the other side that the horses have to be defrosted before you can put their saddles on.

When it gets hot it really gets hot. Old folks used to say that there was only a sheet of greaseproof paper between the Speewah and Hell. With the heat came droughts — these were terrible times and at one point they had to close two lanes of the Municipal Swimming Pool. The Speewah folk would only consider the drought over when they could have water in their tea. One time, it hadn't rained for six years and there were six-year-old frogs that hadn't even learnt to swim! One young boy of a similar age had never seen rain, and when it did finally come down he fainted and they had to throw a bucket of dust in his face to revive him.

Winter was another trial altogether. Old-timers talk of the big freeze being so bad one year that even the mirages froze over. Old Charlie Sutton, the bullocky, tells of one bitterly cold morning when he put his billy on the fire and then went to tend to his bullockies. On his return, the billycan had completely melted, leaving a solid block of ice on the fire. Old Charlie and his mates used to have a fire roaring and when they wanted to have a conversation, they would lean over the fire and wait until the heat melted their frozen words — that was the only way they could talk in that terribly cold country.

Mind you, they don't talk that fast out in Speewah country, so this phenomenon is understandable.

Now, the most famous person in the Speewah district was undoubtedly Crooked Mick. He was a giant of a man who was born way back when the Jenolan Caves were mere wombat holes and the Murray River was a puddle. When he was only nine years old, he weighed twenty-eight stone and was a staggering six feet tall. Understandably, his mother could never keep him in clothes and, out of frustration, she sent him off to the timber town of Wauchope where a couple of timber cutters ringbarked his ankles. That seemed to do the trick for a while, however, he did eventually grow to seven feet three inches.

They reckon Mick had a ferocious appetite and would eat two sheep for breakfast — three if they were weaners — plus three loaves of bread, a tin of plum jam, two dozen eggs and a couple of pints of tea.

When Crooked Mick turned twenty, he applied for a job as a shearer on the nearby Billycandoocandont sheep station. He proved to be a devil of a shearer and worked so hard and fast that he kept a rouseabout full-time just to put ice cubes into a bucket — Mick would make the shears red hot and the bucket was the only way to cool them down. Unfortunately, he was also a messy shearer — bits of blood and ears went in every direction.

The boss came down one morning and, seeing the massacre, screamed at Mick: 'You're bloody well fired!'

Before Mick could slow down and stop, he'd shorn another thirty-two sheep.

After leaving the sheds, he secured a job as a dingo trapper. The wild dogs were not only huge in the Speewah, but bloody clever to boot. Arming himself with ammunition and rifle, Crooked Mick set off for the scrub. At nightfall, he built himself a good campfire and sat in the darkness waiting and watching. After about two hours, he saw them — 200 to 300 pairs of reddish eyes silently watching his every move. Mick was a renowned shooter and he raised his gun and blasted away, taking careful aim to shoot the wild dogs dead centre between the eyes. He reckoned he had killed at least 150 dingoes during that first night, so he curled up close to the fire and slept until dawn.

The next morning he rose and had a dingo shooter's breakfast (a piss, a fart and a good look around) and was off to collect his pelts. There wasn't one single dead dingo to be found. Bloody odd, thought Mick.

The next night he decided to take a mate with him, old Spinner McGroin, the tosser for the Speewah Two-up Society, who was renowned for his 20/20 eyesight. Together they would solve this mystery. At dark they lit a huge fire and Mick loaded his gun and told Spinner to climb high into a gumtree so he had a wide field of vision. Eventually, the dingoes started to howl and to case the campsite. Spinner agreed with Mick that there must have been something like 150 of the devils. The wild dogs started circling the campsite with their eyes glowing as red as blood. One by one, Mick lined up their eyes and fired as quickly as a machine gun until there wasn't a dingo to be seen. Old Spinner McGroin climbed out of the tree looking like he'd seen a ghost.

'Struth!' he spluttered as he came over to Mick. 'You're not gonna believe this, but those dingoes were working in pairs and each dog had its outside eye firmly closed. When you took aim at the point directly between their eyes, you were actually firing between two animals. Talk about bloody cunning bastards!'

It isn't only the dingoes who are clever out in Speewah territory. Most of the wildlife is much bigger and smarter than anywhere else in Australia. Rabbits the size of sheep, giant kangaroos, and wild pigs the size of a Volkswagon. The hoop snakes, the ones that put their tails in their mouths and roll along like hoops, travel at such speed that they often pass cars travelling on the highway. One of the most feared things in the area is the Speewah mossie, and cases have been reported of medium-sized mosquitoes actually blowing out candles so they can commence their bloodthirsty work. Mind you, the medium-sized ones are about the size of a banana. The full-sized mosquitoes are to be feared and have been known to band together to lift blankets off beds and, on at least one occasion, they have been known to steal small dogs.

The real problem for the Speewah farm community is the rabbit. It is as big as sheep and there are millions of the buggers. There was a terrible plague of them back in the thirties, and there wasn't a blade of grass to be seen anywhere in the district — just miles and miles of grey fur as it moved across the land. Apparently, it looked like a sea except you could walk on it like it was a thick carpet. Crooked Mick had been employed by one large property to get rid of the rabbits and he'd tried every trick in the rabbiter's book. He tried poisoning them with myxo, but they seemed to like the taste of the stuff so much that they used to hang around waiting for the next load. He put ferrets into the burrows (he had to push the rabbits out to get the ferrets in), but this didn't work at all — the rabbits must have liked the look of the ferrets because they started to marry them and breed a fiercer rabbit.

After a month he hadn't made a dint in the plague and, as he got up one morning, he noticed that the rabbits had started to get organised — they were all standing very close together, ready for a final attack on the station and, it seemed, on Crooked Mick. He grabbed a full bottle of Bundaberg rum and downed the lot, reasoning that he would go down fighting. And attack they did, millions of them. They tumbled Crooked Mick up into the sky and he was being carried along by a sea of fur when, as it does in that part of the world, a most peculiar thing happened. One of those 'cold snaps' moved in and froze every one of those darned rabbits there and then.

When asked why he didn't freeze too, Crooked Mick just laughed.

'Oh, it was the rum that saved me. Anyway,' he continued, 'I was given a hand by a passing bloke, a Yank tourist named Bill Bird's Eye, who witnessed the event and then purchased the entire lot. Apparently, he packaged them and shipped them off to California where he sold them as: "Snap-frozen Underground Mutton". I hear he made a fortune out of the deal.'

Crooked Mick's next job was as a drover, but he didn't like the long riding days. His most notable assignment is a toss up between the time he had to drive 3000 Murray cod across the Nullarbor Plains (he never lost a scale), and the time he had to take 20 000 camels and their Afghan drivers down to Sydney's Pitt Street Mall.

There are very few women in Speewah. They tend not to like the climate and, besides, the local water is far too hard for them. The water is often so hard that it needs to be chopped with an axe before you can use it.

One of the most celebrated women in Speewah would have to be Prickly Pear Poll — a notoriously ugly woman who had a face not unlike a prickly pear. Poll had the 'hots' for Crooked Mick and said she 'would follow him to the end of the earth'. One time she did follow him as far down as the Riverina. So desperate was she to get near Mick, she asked the station boss of his shed if he had any work for her.

'No, sorry, Poll, nothing here.'

But she would not give up easily, and day after day she returned to pester the man. Finally, he gave in when she offered to 'scare off the crows' from his corn fields but he had to sack her after only two days. She'd frightened the poor crows so much that they went home and returned all the corn they'd pinched over the past three months. Prickly Pear Poll was that ugly!

Another memorable Speewah character was 'Greasy George', the shearer's cook. You couldn't even look at George because your eyes would slip right off him — he was that greasy! They reckoned George had a bath once a year, but not in a leap year.

Another local was Bungeye Bill, the Speewah gambler. They used to say he'd bet on anything: two flies on a wall (which one will buzz off first?), a dog scratching fleas (which leg will he use?) and, of course, two-up. They said he had plenty of brains but not enough sense to use them!

FROM THE TRENCHES

Australia has fought in twelve wars, from the so-called Maori Wars of the 1860s to the Timor War, and the Australian Digger has a well-deserved reputation as an honourable and tenacious fighter. Our Diggers also have a reputation as independent thinkers, and this is brought out in military humour.

War is always a horrible thing and humour in songs, poetry and yarns plays an important role in defusing emotions — especially stress and frustration. How else can recruits retaliate against the endless screaming of the sergeant major other than by making light of their situation?

Like those of the shearing sheds the army cook comes in for a fair beating, as does most forms of authority — especially the 'top brass'.

THE TATTOOED LADY

I paid a franc to see a fair tattooed lad-y,

And right across her jaw, were the words 'great Anzac Corp'.

And on her chest was a possum, and a great big kangaroo,

And on her back was a Union Jack, coloured red, white and blue.

A map of Germany, was where I couldn't see,

And right across her hips, was a line of battleships.

And on her kidney, and on her kidney,

Was a bird's-eye view of Sydney.

And 'round the corner, 'round the corner,

Was my home in Woolloomooloo.

(Traditional song from the singing of Mossy Phillips)

BUGGER OFF!

There was a certain Australian drill sergeant major who gave his commands in a most unorthodox manner.

'Slope arms! You too!'

'Present arms! You too!'

'Forward arms! You too!'

'Forward march! You too!'

One day, after the parade, a young lieutenant approached the sar' major and asked him to explain his unusual commands.

'Well, sir,' he replied, 'it's like this: these men are tough bastards, and every time I give an order I know they're going to tell me to bugger off — and I prefer to beat them to it.'

PONSOMBURY

The two retired British Army officers were enjoying a quiet 'spot' at the club when one turned to the other to enquired: 'Whatever happened to Ponsombury?'

'Ponsombury,' replied the other haughtily. 'I believe he stayed on in India. Married a damned gorilla — big hairy thing it was, too!'

'Good God, man!' exclaimed the other in total amazement. 'Look, I have to ask this, but was it a male or a female gorilla?'

'A female, of course — nothing queer about Ponsombury!'

The infantry, the infantry,
With the mud behind their ears;
The infantry, the infantry,
Can drink their weight in beers.

The cavalry, artillery,
and the dog-gone engineers,
Oh, they couldn't lick the infantry,
In a hundred thousand years.

HIS OLD MAN OWNS A PUB

The Australian soldiers had been in the Middle East for months and going stir-crazy with the heat and dust. During one of the regular route marches across the desert, the troop stopped for a smoko. As the platoon captain did his rounds, he noticed a young soldier huddled in a corner nursing his head in his hands and sobbing quietly.

'What's the matter with your mate?' the captain enquired of a nearby soldier.

'Homesickness, sir,' replied the soldier.

'Oh,' said the captain, 'guess we all suffer from that at times.'

'Yes, but this one's got it real bad,' said the soldier. 'His old man owns a pub.'

Oh, the colonel kicks the major,
Then the major has a go,
He kicks the poor old captain,
Who then kicks the NCO.
And as the kicks get harder,
They are passed on down to me.
And I am kicked to bleeding hell,
To save democracy.

LONG CALL

A Yank soldier 'put one up' on a Digger about a famous echo in America.

'If one were to call out at 11.00 a.m., the echo wouldn't be heard 'till three o'clock that afternoon.'

'That's nothing,' said the Digger. 'Why, in Australia we sounded the bugle call in 1914, but youse blokes didn't hear it until 1917.'

DIGGER

Digger: 'Quartermaster, these bloody army pants are no good. They're tighter than my skin!'

Quartermaster: 'Come on soldier, how th' blazes can they be tighter than your skin?'

Digger: 'Well, I can sit in my skin but I'm blowed if I can sit in these duds.'

SAR' MAJOR

'Well, soldier,' snarled the tough old sar' major to the private, 'I suppose after you are discharged from the army, you'll just be waiting for me to die so you can spit on my grave?'

'No bloody way, Sarge,' the private assured the snarling man. 'Once I'm out of this platoon, I'm never going to queue again.'

ON PARADE

The sar' major was calling the roll on parade.

'Johnson!'

'Yair,' drawled Johnson.

'Simpson!'

''ere,' was the somewhat reluctant response.

'Jackson!'

'She's sweet,' came an echo.

'Smith!'

'Here, sir!'

'Bloody crawler!' shouted the entire platoon.

HOW'D YOU BE?

I struck him first in a shearing shed in outback Queensland. He was sweating over a greasy four-year-old wether when I asked him the innocent question: 'How would yer be?'

He didn't answer immediately, but waited until he had carved the last bit of wool from the struggling sheep, allowed the animal to regain its feet, kicked it through the chute, dropped the shears, and spat what looked like a stream of molten metal about three yards. Then he fixed on me a pair of eyes in which the fires of a deep hatred seemed to burn — he pierced me with them — and he said: 'How would I be? How the bloody hell would you expect me to be? Get a hold of me, will ya! Dags on every inch of my bloody hide; drinking me own bloody sweat; swallowing dirt with every bloody breath I breathe; working for the lousiest bastard this side of the rabbit-proof bloody fence and frightened to leave here because the old woman has got some bloody private Dick Tracy looking for me with a bloody maintenance order. How would I be? I'm so bloody unlucky they could be showing free movies up a sheep's bum and I'd still be some poor dag hanging around the back! I haven't tasted beer for weeks and the last glass I had was knocked over by some clumsy drunken bastard before I got a chance to finish it! How would you bloody well expect me to be!'

The next time I saw him was in Sydney down at Circular Quay. He was struggling to get into a set of regulation Army webbing and had almost ruptured himself in the process. I strolled up and said: 'How would you be, Digger?'

'How would I bloody well be?' he responded. 'Take a bloody gander at me! Get a load of this bloody outfit; take a bloody Captain Cook at this bloody hat — size nine and a half and I take a seven — my bloody ears are the only thing holding it up; and get an eyeful of these strides, why you could hide a bloody bullock team in the arse of them and still have room for me; get an eyeful of this shirt, just get on the bloody thing, will you! Look at these bloody daisy roots — there's enough boot leather in the bastards to make a full set of saddle and harness! And then some know-it-all bastard told me this was a "man's outfit"! How would I be? How the bloody hell would you expect me to be!'

I next saw him on the front line at Tobruk. He was seated on an upturned ammo box, tin hat over one eye, cigarette butt hanging from his bottom lip, rifle leaning against one knee, and he was trying to clean his nails with the tip of his bayonet. I should have known better, but I couldn't help but ask him: 'How would you be, Digger?'

He swallowed the dodger butt as the bayonet sliced off the top of his index finger, and he fixed me with a murderous stare. 'How would I be? How would I bloody well be? How the bloody hell would you bloody expect me to be? Six months in this hell hole, being target practice for every Fritz in kingdom come; eating bloody sand with every meal; flies in my hair and eyes; lice in every bloody crevice and crease on my body; too frightened to sleep a bloody wink, expecting to die in this bloody place and copping the crows every time there's a handout to anybody! How would I be? How the bloody hell would you expect me to be?'

The last time I saw him was in Heaven. I know I should have kept on flying but I ventured a cheery: 'How would you be, cobber?'

He pierced me with an unholy look that riveted my soul as he fluttered and muttered: 'How would I be? How the bloody Heaven would I be? Get a grip on this bloody regulation nightgown would you? A man trips over the bloody thing fifty times a day and it takes a cove ten minutes to lift the bloody thing just to relieve himself; and get a gander at this bloody right wing — feathers missing all over the darned thing — a man might be bloody well moulting! Get an eyeful of this halo, only my ears keep the rotten thing on my skull — and look at the bloody dents in it — it's obviously secondhand! How would I bloody well be? Cast your eyes on this celestial bloody harp: five bloody strings missing and there's a bloody band practice in six minutes. How would I be, you ask? How would you expect a man to bloody well be!'

DAD
AND DAVE

Dad, Mum, Dave and Mabel were all characters in Steele Rudd's *On Our Selection*, which still stands as one of Australia's most hilarious books of bush humour. It was also made into a feature film and has seen the recent light of day as a play. What Rudd most probably didn't expect was for his characters to assume their own life in folklore. A fine compliment indeed! Dad and Dave yarns still thrive across Australia. Often bawdy, sometimes sexist and nearly always funny, the yarns see the various members of the Rudd family thrown into improbable situations. Long may they make us laugh at ourselves.

LIGHTS OUT

Dad was having a quiet beer in the local rubbity-dub when in walks Dave looking very down in the mouth.

'Dave, what'ya doin' here? I thought ya waz goin' out with Mabel tonight?'

'I was. I went round to her place and everything and then she starts to turn out all the lights. I can take a hint, so I left.'

I'VE ALWAYS WANTED TO DO THAT

Dad and Dave were walking through the bush when all of a sudden, Dave signalled Dad to stop and be quiet.

'Shhh. Look Dad, through there, see that dingo?'

Dad peered through the scrub and sure enough, there was a dingo busily licking his testicles.

Dave whispered to Dad: 'I've always wanted to do that.'

Dad looked at Dave in a weird way and said: 'Well, Dave, I'd suggest you pat him first!'

THE TALES OF HOFFMANN

Dave was on his very first visit to Sydney and, being the Depression, rationing was in full swing. Before he made tracks for the big smoke, Dad had given Dave some sound advice on how to cope with the city: 'If you want anything to eat, you'll have to get in a queue.'

Dave, like most bushmen, found the city bewildering but he was determined to make the best of a bad situation. On his second night, he was wandering idly when he came across a long queue of people outside a brightly lit building. Being hungry, he recalled Dad's advice and joined the queue.

After shuffling along for half an hour, he began to get bored. He shook the arm of the fur-coated woman in front of him.

'Eh,' he said, 'do yer know what's on up there, missus?'

'Tales of Hoffmann,' said the woman as she superciliously snubbed her nose at the bushman.

'Aw, well,' said Dave, 'I've lived most of my life on kangaroo tail soup and wallaby tail stew. Might as well wait and git somethin' different for tea — no 'arm in trying somethin' new.'

TAKE WHAT YOU WANT

Dad and Dave were headed for town when they noticed a pretty girl on the side of the road trying to mend a broken bicycle chain. Dave winked at Dad and said he'd catch up with him at the Royal Hotel just as soon as he fixed the young lady's pushbike. An hour later, Dave arrives at the hotel riding the bicycle.

Says Dad: 'Dave, how come you're riding the bicycle?'

'Well,' said Dave with a smug look on his dial, 'I fixed the bike chain and the young lady looked at me and pulled her panties right down and said: "Take what you want!" Well, I took the bicycle!'

Dad thought about this and scratched his long beard. 'Probably a good thing 'cause the panties wouldn't 'ave fit yer anyway.'

NAKED AMBITION

Dave was wandering down the main street of town when the local copper spotted him.

'Hey! Dave! What the hell do you think you're doing walking in town stark bloody naked?'

Dave looked at the policemen and started to explain that he'd been riding the boundary fences when a young woman stepped out from behind a tree pointing a gun at him.

'She told me to get down off my horse and she shooed it off, and then told me to take off all my clothes. After I was naked, she took all her clothes off and told me to "go to town". I wasn't going to argue with a woman with a loaded gun.'

STEAK AND EGGS

Dad and Dave were travelling out west and were hankering for a decent meal when they decided to stop at a small country town. They sank a few beers in the public bar and then fronted the barman about where they could get a decent meal in town.

'Well, fellows, there's the pub or the pub but the menu is fairly limited. There's steak and onions or steak and eggs.'

'We'll have the steak and onions,' chorused Dad and Dave and they returned to drinking their beers.

The meal arrived and they both got stuck into the steak but after a couple of mouthfuls they both gagged and Dave, despite being ravenous, threw his steak onto the floor in disgust.

'That's got to be the most foul-tasting food I've ever eaten,' Dave said.

The pub's resident dog started to gulp down the steak. The barman gestured towards the dog, and sarcastically said: 'I don't know where you blokes come from, but the dog seems to think it's okay to eat.'

'Sure, he's eating it alright,' said Dad, 'but look at the way he has to keep licking his arse to get the bad taste out of his mouth!'

BRIDAL SUITE?

The time had come for Dave and Mabel to get married and they decided to have their honeymoon in Brisbane. Dave, grinning like a coot, told the desk clerk: 'I'd like a nice room for the night for our honeymoon.'

'Of course,' said the receptionist. 'Bridal suite?'

'Ahh, no thanks miss, I'll just hang onto her ears.'

MAKING BACON

Dad and Dave decided that they needed to diversify their farm and had heard that pork was getting good returns. They didn't know anything about raising pigs other than what they learnt from the promotional leaflet, which told them that they needed a fertile sow which would deliver piglets after she was 'serviced'.

They purchased a good sow and asked around Snake Gully to see who had boars. Luckily their neighbour had a number of boars, so they placed their sow in a wheelbarrow and off they went.

When they reached the neighbouring property, the farmer said: 'I've got three boars for the job, there's a five-pound boar, a ten-pound boar and my twenty-pound boar'

'Since we're just starting out,' Dad offered, 'we'll have the five-pound boar.'

The next morning, Dave looks in the sty expecting to see the sow with piglets, but there's nothing there but the sow.

'Dad,' said an anxious Dave, 'it didn't seem to work — there are no piglets.'

Dad looked in and said: 'Maybe we should've used the ten-pound boar.'

So they placed the sow in the wheelbarrow again and off they went to the farmer.

'We'd better try the ten-pounder.'

Next morning, Dave leaps up and races out to the sty but no piglets — just the old sow.

'Dad, it didn't work.'

'Hmmm, maybe we should have used the twenty-pound boar and saved all the trouble.'

They placed the sow in the wheelbarrow and off they went again.

Next morning Dave, confident that this time they'd have a litter of piglets, looked into the sty but there were no piglets and even the old sow was missing.

He looked out of the barn and saw the sow sitting in the wheelbarrow.

SOUNDS GOOD TO ME

Dave comes rushing into the house to tell Mum and Dad the news.

'There's a new pub opened in Snake Gully. And for a quid, you get one of those new light beers, then they take you out the back and you get a root.'

'Is that so,' says Dad, 'are you sure about this, Dave?'

'Sure am.'

'Have you tried it?'

'No, Dad, but Mabel has.'

FOWL'OUSE DISASTER

Dave had promised to meet Mabel at 7.00 a.m. on Saturday morning. But when he finally arrived, he was two hours late. Mabel, hopping mad, set forth a string of abuse and was in the middle of giving Dave a good dressing down when he interrupted her.

'Mabel! Calm down! I know I'm late but, honestly, it wasn't my fault.'

She looked at him suspiciously. 'Well, what's yer excuse?'

'It was like this,' commenced Dave. 'Mum thought she 'eard someone in the fowl'ouse last night so she woke Dad and made him get 'is shotgun and go out and look. Just as he pointed the gun at the fowl'ouse, I come runnin' up behind with the pitchfork, and yer know how fast I can run, Mabel — well, we've been cleanin' fowls since 4.00 a.m. this morning.'

BUSH VIAGRA

Dad was very worried about his cows. Every time he led the bull into the paddock, it would ignore the herd and just eat the grass. This went on for days until, one morning, the bull was so impatient to get into the paddock that it was almost uncontrollable. When it did get amongst the cows, it serviced every one of them — twice. Dad was beaming that night when he told Dave the good news.

Dave smiled at Dad and said: 'Thought it might do the trick.'

'What'd'yer mean?' enquired Dad.

'Well, I gave the cows some of that liquid stuff in the back of the barn.'

Dad looked at Dave and said: 'What liquid stuff?'

'I don't know what it is,' Dave said, smiling, 'but it has a sort of peppermint taste.'

THAT'S MY BABY

Dave was heading down to the city in Snake Gully's only taxi. When they reached the railway junction, the driver offered Dave some homely advice.

'You be careful down in the city, Dave. There's some loose women in that town.'

'Don't you worry about me,' said Dave. 'I'm no fool.'

A fortnight later, he was back and the taxi was waiting and ready for the homeward trip.

'Hang on,' says Dave, 'we've got to make room for my wife.'

The taxi driver couldn't help but notice that the young girl standing on the railway platform was about six months pregnant.

'Dave, how could that women be your wife when she's going to have a baby and it's obviously not yours.'

'Of course it's my baby,' protested Dave.

'How d'yer reckon it's your baby?'

'Well,' said Dave, 'if you buy a cow and it has a calf, the calf's yours, ain't it?'

CITY SLICKER IN THE DAM

Dad and Mum were in the kitchen when Dave came running up to the house.

'Dad! Dad! There's one of those city blokes down in the dam.'

'What's he doin' son?' asked Dad.

'Drowning,' said Dave.

A LONG DISTANCE TO SYDNEY

Dad, Mum and Dave were sitting around the kitchen table having a cup of tea when the telephone rang. Dave sauntered over to the phone, answered it and then put the receiver back as he laughed.

'Gawd, those city people are practical jokers. One of them just called to say it wuz a long distance from Sydney!'

LAZY LEN

Australian workers are rarely lazy but Lazy Len takes the cake, and is most probably lazy on behalf of us all. Maybe he was the original 'Norm'?

SNAKE

Lazy Len lay basking in the midday sun behind the pub when a passer-by saw a tiger snake sliding dangerously close to his feet.

'Watch out there, mate!' he shouted. 'There's a "Joe Blake" near your foot and it looks angry.'

Lazy Len continued to bask in the warm sunlight. 'Which foot, mate?' he asked, yawning.

HE WAS THAT LAZY

Lazy Len used to set his alarm so he could get up an hour early so he could have an extra hour to be lazy. He was that lazy!

When Lazy Len saw a pretty girl in town he blew kisses — he was that lazy!

Lazy Len was so lazy he was waiting for the Bible to come out in paperback!

Lazy Len got into the habit of breaking his cigarettes in two so he didn't have to draw so hard. He was that lazy!

Lazy Len made his cow eat a whole calendar so he could have cream-covered dates. He was that lazy!

Lazy Len once lived in a boarding house in Sydney and instead of table napkins he used to wipe his greasy hands on the dog's back. Every week they'd wash the dog and use the water for soup. He was that lazy!

APRICOT BLOODY JAM

'Bloody apricot jam sandwiches again,' spat a disgusted Lazy Len, as he opened his lunch box.

The next day and for the rest of the week, he complained about the apricot jam sandwiches.

Sick of his moaning, one of the men leant across and suggested: 'Len, why don't you ask your wife to make something different?'

'I can't,' whinged Lazy Len. 'I make my own lunch!'

LAZY LEN AND THE ARMY

The fellows were discussing how lazy Lazy Len was when one bloke suggested that what Len needed was a spell in the army.

'Nar, they'd never take him in the army — he's too short.'

'How d'ya know?' replied another. 'Has anyone ever seen him stand up?'

SPAGHETTI

Lazy Len stumbled into work with bandages on both feet up to his ankles.

'What on earth happened to you?' his workmates wanted to know.

'Well,' said Len, 'for a start, I'm never going to eat spaghetti again!'

His mates looked puzzled until Lazy Len explained: 'I took a tin of spaghetti from the pantry and the directions on the can said: "Stand in boiling water for ten minutes."'

LAZY LEN AND NED KELLY'S SKULL

Lazy Len was trying to make a few extra quid at the local show day by exhibiting a few artefacts he had picked up on his travels.

He held up a few and then enticed people to join him in the small tent to see the real valuables. He held up a skull and declared: 'Ladies and gentlemen, this here is the skull of the great bushranger Ned Kelly.'

'Come off it,' one of the squatters screamed out. 'That's far too small to be Ned Kelly's skull.'

Lazy Len didn't lift an eyebrow as he looked the man in the face. 'Fool. This is the head of Ned Kelly as a boy!'

NOT MUCH WIND

Lazy Len got a job helping a cow cocky build a second windmill on his property.

'Are you sure you want another one?' Lazy Len questioned.

'Why'd ya ask?' said the cocky.

'Well, I noticed there's hardly enough wind to blow the one you've got, let alone two!'

THE HEADACHE

Lazy Len went to see his doctor for a check-up and to find out why he had a constant headache.

'Hmm,' said the doctor, 'I'm having a bit of difficulty diagnosing your problem, but I think it's just a hangover.'

'I understand, Doc,' said Lazy Len. 'I'll come back when you sober up!'

RABBITS

Rabbits hot; rabbits cold;
Rabbits young; rabbits old;
Rabbits fat; rabbits lean;
Rabbits dirty; rabbits clean;
Rabbits big; rabbits small;
Rabbits short; rabbits tall;
Rabbits black; rabbits white;

Rabbits for breakfast; rabbits at night;
Rabbits stewed; rabbits roast;
Rabbits on gravy; rabbits on toast;
Rabbits by the dozen; rabbits by the score;
Rabbits tender; rabbits tough;
Lord, spare me from rabbits;
I've had enough!

WHY THERE'S NO GRASS IN THE OUTBACK

There's a good reason why there's no grass in the outback. Years ago, a squatter imported a couple of rabbits as pets for his kids and, rabbits being rabbits, they started to have little rabbits. Lots of little rabbits. One day it became very obvious that he would have to do something because his whole station was covered with rabbits, thousands of the buggers, and they just kept on breeding. He talked to his head stockman and told him to get rid of them.

'Jeez, Boss, where the hell am I gonna take them?'

The boss thought about it and told the head stockman that the only thing was to treat 'em like sheep.

'Round 'em up and get a couple of dingoes as sheep dogs. Drive 'em up north where there's plenty of open land. Keep 'em moving until you're way up near Darwin and they won't remember where they were raised.'

They spent two months training the dingoes and rounding up the bunny mob and one day they were gone.

That's why there's no grass in the outback — the bloody rabbits ate it all when they were moving up north.

He was lazy

He was cheeky

He was dirty

He was sly

But he had a single virtue

And its name was rabbit pie!

CLEVER, THOSE RABBITS

The old bloke had been sent out to shoot some pigeons so his wife could bake up a pie. There he was, sitting under a convenient coolabah tree, down by the old reservoir, gun in hand. The reservoir was fenced off with barbed wire and the water level was extremely low for the time of year. As he sat staring up at the sky, he glanced down and saw a large buck rabbit moving towards him. The rabbit circled the fence looking for an opening to get through to reach the water, but it wasn't possible. He sat there staring at the water for a good ten minutes before he bolted off into the bush and started scratching around. The old bushman was intrigued when he saw the rabbit return with a long piece of dried sow thistle, but he was totally amazed when he saw the rabbit slide the straw through the fence and into the reservoir and take a long, long drink of water. He never did get those pigeons and didn't have the heart to shoot such a smart rabbit.

GOOD MATHS

Dave was caught holding a rabbit by the neck and violently smacking it as he recited: 'Seven by seven, ten by ten, twelve by ten.'

Mabel was looking on curiously. 'What ya doing that for, Dave?'

Dave stopped and put the rabbit down. 'Arrh, Mabel, I just wanted to see if it was true that rabbits multiply rapidly, but they don't.'

WORKING
LIFE

Folklore comes in so many forms and it is important that it be seen as part of a living tradition and not simply as something from the past. We all create and pass on folklore, mostly unconsciously, and the workplace is just another opportunity for us to document our lives through story-telling. One of the most active areas related to workplace lore is that of nicknames. Australians love to pin nicknames on each other. An old mate of mine, Harry Stein, used to collect nicknames for me from down at the wharves where he worked. Some of them were beauties:

'The Judge' — was always sitting on a case.

'Hydraulic' — he'd lift anything.

'The Barrister' — spent so much time at the bar.

'The Dog' — used to call everyone 'Pal'.

'Preserved Peaches' — always in the can.

'Singlets' — the boss who was always on the worker's backs.

'Crocodile' — always biting mates for a loan.

'The Undertaker' — always sizing you up.

Then there's the tradition of 'first-day pranks' where new chums, often apprentices, are sent out for impossible objects or targeted to be sent up. In many cases, everyone else knows about the joke except the poor individual.

Plumbers are dispatched to the local hardware store for a 'long weight' and the store staff simply instruct him to 'wait here' and he does! Nurses are often sent to the hospital store to request 'fallopian tubes'. Carpenters are sent for 'a dozen sky hooks'. Bricklayers are sent for a 'right-hand trowel'. Accountants are sent for 'scales to balance the books' and young lawyers are sent for 'verbal agreement forms'.

UNION DOGS

Four union delegates were discussing how clever their dogs were.

The first was a delegate for the Vehicle Workers Union who declared that his dog could do mathematical calculations and its name was 'T-square'. He told T-square to go to the blackboard and draw a square, a circle and a triangle, which the dog did with considerable ease.

The Amalgamated Metalworkers Union delegate said that his dog was smarter and that its name was 'Slide Rule'. He told the dog to fetch a dozen dog biscuits and divide them into four piles, which the dog did in two minutes flat.

The Liquor Trades delegate admitted that both dogs were impressive but his dog, called 'Measure', could outshine and outsmart them both. He told his dog to go and fetch a stubbie of beer and pour seven ounces into a ten-ounce glass. The dog did this without flicking an ear.

They turned to the Maritime Workers Union delegate and asked what his dog could do to beat that, but before they could smirk, he whistled for his dog 'Tea Break' and told him to 'Show these bastards what you can do.'

Tea Break shuffled up and ate the biscuits, drank the beer, pissed on the blackboard, screwed the three other dogs, claimed he injured his back, filled out a worker's compensation claim and shot through on sick leave.

BIBLE SCHOLAR

The shearer had tickets on himself as a Bible scholar and was always boasting that he could recite, word perfect, the Lord's Prayer. One of his fellow workers, tired of the continual boasting, bet him ten dollars he didn't know it.

'I'll show you,' he replied and off he went. 'Here with a loaf of bread beneath the bough, a flask of wine, a book of verse and thou beside me singing in the wilderness.'

His mate looked on in amazement as he handed over the ten dollars. 'I could have sworn he didn't know it.'

THE GANDER AND THE POM

In a northern New South Wales town there lived an Englishman who earned his crust by doing odd jobs. He was fairly well known and had taken a job with a woman who bred geese on a small farm just outside of town. Like a lot of Poms in those days, he took to wearing big baggy shorts known as 'Bombay bloomers'. Well, on this day, he was nailing timber on the back shed and, as usual, there were geese walking all over the place and one of them obviously saw something tasty dangling down inside his shorts — so he decided to swallow it! The surprised Pom threw down his hammer in horror and grabbed the goose by the neck, shaking the poor bird so he could get his you-know-what back. Well, this proved to be rather difficult as a gander's teeth slope backwards. After a brief and bitter struggle, the man was forced to yell for help from the old woman. He was getting very worried because the gander showed absolutely no indication of giving the man his property back.

The woman tried to help but didn't know where to start or what to grab hold of, so she said: 'It's no use — I'll have to go into the house and fetch a carving knife and cut its throat.'

At this point, the desperate man screamed: 'For Christ sake, don't do that! I don't know how much he's got down his throat!'

Eventually, the woman decided to choke the gander to death and this worked, but the man's penis was badly scratched and cut. She drove him into the town hospital, where the local doctors had to give him several stitches. The whole episode created much talk and amusement in the town and it was indeed a very sore point for the Pom.

THE CUSTOMER

A shop assistant got sick of being polite to rude customers and he was always getting into trouble with his boss, who continually reminded him that the customer was always right.

One day, the boss was startled to see the shop assistant walking down the street in a policeman's uniform.

'Why did you become a police officer?' he asked.

'Well,' he replied, 'I joined the force when they told me that the policeman's motto is: the customer is always wrong!'

PRIVATE

A group of miners had finished their daily shift and were showering off the pitch black coal soot. Noticing that Ernie was missing, they saw that he was hiding coyly behind the lockers with a towel covering his private parts.

'Why so coy, Ernie?' asked one of the miners.

'Well, you see,' said Ernie, 'you can't be too careful these days, because when any government sees anything big they immediately want to privatise it!'

WORLDLY THOUGHTS

Bill the drover had reached the age of fifty and had never owned a suit. He'd even gotten married in a rented tuxedo. His thirtieth wedding anniversary was approaching, so he decided to get the best tailor in Australia to make him a suit for the celebration.

The tailor showed him an enormous range of cloth and after selecting a nice length of grey wool, the tailor started to measure him up for the suit. Bill chattered away, saying how pleased he was to have the best tailor in the country making his first suit and how proud he would be in four weeks when he arrived at the anniversary party.

The tailor looked up and snapped: 'That settles it! I cannot make your suit.'

Bill stared back in amazement. 'But that's ridiculous,' complained Bill. 'I've selected the cloth, you've measured me and you're the best tailor in Australia.'

The tailor looked at Bill and explained. 'It is because I am the best tailor in the country that I cannot make your suit — I simply cannot make a suit in four weeks.'

'But,' spluttered Bill, 'the good Lord made the world in seven days, yet it takes you more than four weeks to make a suit?'

'Yes,' replied the tailor, 'but have you had a good look at the world lately?'

BULLOCKIES

The bullock driver and his team played an important role in developing rural Australia and, sadly, it is a job of the past. Today's timber industry has massive trucks and chains that rip the giant trees from the soil. The old bullock days certainly produced a lot more folklore than the screaming chainsaw. However, if tradition can be believed, they were just as loud. It has been said that the bullockies were the loudest and most talented users of swear words in the entire world. I'm not sure if this is true, but there are many yarns that point in that noisy direction.

PARROT FASHION

The bush missionary had travelled over a lot of Australia, and here he was riding his buggy along an excuse for a road in the Queensland backblocks when in front of him appeared a bullock team with a load of sleeper rails. He couldn't get past and it was obvious that the bullocky hadn't seen him, besides, there was a flow of the most vulgar and violent language coming from the front of the team. He walked around to the front, but hard as he looked he couldn't see anyone, yet the foul language continued to assail the air. He tried cooeeing but no response came except for more bad language. The only thing he could find was a bright green parrot sitting on the furthest bullock's back.

The parson, mystified, shrugged his shoulders and managed to pass the team, continuing on his journey until he reached a small settlement which offered nothing more than a few houses, a post office and a hotel. He noticed two men lazily seated on the hotel verandah drinking beers, so he decided to investigate.

'There's a bullock team about twenty miles back, completely unattended. I looked for its driver in vain.'

'Thanks, parson,' said the lean, long one, 'you needn't worry. That's my team but, to tell you the truth, it ain't completely unattended.'

'Well,' said the preacher doubtfully, 'I didn't see a soul for miles, the only thing I saw was a green parrot perched on the back of one of your polars.'

'Ah,' said the bullocky with a certain knowing pride, 'that's Percy, me South American parrot. I trained him meself and he's one of the best. In fact, he doesn't even need me.'

'Pity about his language,' sighed the parson. 'Never heard such filthy language in my entire life.'

The bullock driver slammed down his beer glass, clearly annoyed.

'Why, that good fer nothing little feathered bastard!' he roared. 'I told him never to swear in front of ladies or preachers. He'll get the sack when he gets back, that's for bloody sure!'

I KNOW, I KNOW

The bullock driver couldn't help but notice the old man trying to pull a dead horse along the road.

'What on earth are you doing?' he asked of the old man.

'Well, if you really want to know, I could do with a bit of help. I'm trying to get this dead horse up to my property just up the hill.'

The bullocky tethered his team and started to help the old bloke push the dead horse up the hill.

When they got to the steps of the house, the old bloke asked: 'Do you think you could help me get the horse up onto the verandah?'

The bullocky was intrigued and agreed, but when they had the horse on the verandah the old-timer asked if he'd help push him along the hallway. Once again the bullocky agreed.

As he was about to bid farewell to the old-timer he said: 'You must have really loved this old horse.'

The old bloke just looked at the bullocky and said: 'Look, you've been very helpful, but can I ask you one final favour? Can you help me take the horse into the bathroom and sit him up on the toilet?'

This was the final straw for the bullocky, who was just about exploding with curiosity. 'I'll help you if you'll tell me why you've gone to all this bloody trouble.'

The old-timer looked at him and whispered: 'My brother's coming home soon and for thirty-five years I've had to put up with him saying: "I know, I know" every time I tell him something. He's going to take a piss and come in here tonight saying: "There's a bloody horse sitting on the toilet." And I'm going to say: "I know, I know."'

BLOODY STUBBORN BULLOCKS

Cecil the bullocky had been boss of his own team for many years. His team knew every slippery track and road where timber grew and his leader bullock, Old Tremone, was as staunch as they were made. The polars, on the other hand, were a pair of beasts that would baulk at any opportunity.

One day a neighbour, hearing a terrible hullabaloo drifting up from the direction of the dry river bed, went down to investigate. There was Cecil, blue in the face, shouting and cursing at Old Tremone.

'Come on, move yer fat arse, yer rotten old bastard!' he shouted as he flayed the poor animal with a whip.

Old Tremone was obviously straining every ounce of muscle, while the polars just tossed their heads and refused to take any interest in the proceedings.

The neighbour, alarmed at Cecil's treatment of his favourite bullock, shouted: 'Cecil, what the 'ell are you hittin' 'im for?'

'Well, it's no bloody good flogging those other two lazy bastards,' said the bullocky, 'they wouldn't pull the hat off yer head!'

DEARLY DEPARTED

It's only appropriate that the last section in this collection be about the afterlife — Australian style!

GAWD'S STRUTH!

St Peter was suffering from a terrible hangover and asked Jesus if he could have a couple of days off.

'Sure, Peter, but you'll have to give me a few clues as I'm not very experienced in this job.'

'Oh, don't worry,' said St Peter, 'it's as easy as falling off a log. All you've got to do is stand at the gates and look pious and every time someone comes along you ask them to tell you something good they've done on Earth, then you make a decision of whether they come in or go down to Hell.'

So, Jesus was on the door and doing fine until an old man arrived.

'Welcome to Heaven's Gate, tell me something about yourself, old man.'

'Well, I haven't got much of a story. I was a very ordinary man, a good carpenter and that's about it.'

Jesus looked at the old man, remembering Peter's instructions, and continued to quiz him. 'Surely you did something special, something worthwhile?'

'Oh yes, I guess there was one thing — I had a truly remarkable son. Very clever and much-loved throughout the world.'

At this, Jesus, with tears in his eyes, leapt up and hugged the old man as he cried: 'Father, Father, it's me, your son.'

The old man looked up and he, too, started to cry as he yelled out: 'Pinocchio?'

LOOKING GOOD

Dan had been sick for ages and finally carked it after a six-month stay in the local hospital. His long-time mates decided the least they could do was to attend the funeral and to pay their last respects.

They filed past the open casket and wished the old bloke a fond farewell and then headed to the local pub.

'The old bastard looked pretty good, didn't he?'

'And so he should have,' replied his fellow drinker. 'He's just come out of hospital.'

RELIGION

The Pope had died and a new pontiff had to be elected.

'Who do you think should be the next pope?' asked a shearer of his mates in the hut.

'Cardinal Spellman of New York,' shouted a Yank.

'T'would be about time we had an Irishman,' suggested Paddy O'Doyle.

'I reckon it should be Cardinal "Bluey" Gilmore from St Mary's in Sydney,' said Mick Ryan.

A shearer up the back looked up from his book and shouted: 'Bob Menzies, of course!'

A silence fell over the group until the original questioner piped up, saying: 'But Menzies isn't even a Catholic.'

'Oh well,' said the worm, sinking back into his book, 'if you're going to bring religion into it.'

NO PAPER

A man went into the church confessional and waited and waited until he could wait no more. He commenced to knock on the priest's wall, thinking the priest had accidentally fallen asleep.

'No use making that racket, mate, there's no toilet paper in here either!' was the innocent reply.

THE SWAGGIES AT THE GATES OF HEAVEN

Three swag-carriers arrived at the Pearly Gates on Christmas Eve, where St Peter confronted them.

'What have we here? Three swaggies, eh? I tell you what: I'll ignore the "snowdropping"; the petty thievery and the bad language on one condition — that you each give me something Christmasy!'

'Struth!' they all cried, 'that's a bloody hard bargain.'

The first swaggie reached into his pocket and pulled out a crumpled and dirty Christmas card from his sister and he handed it to St Peter.

'It's not much, however, it is a Christmas card alright!'

'Enter!' declared the Gate Keeper.

The next swaggie looked a bit doubtful as he reached into his swag and pulled out a mouldy piece of ancient-looking fruitcake.

'It's a Christmas cake! A bit old, and to tell you the truth, it's made out of baked beans, it doesn't taste too good but it can blow out its own candles!'

St Peter, not one to have the wool pulled over his eyes, reckoned that the swaggie could enter on the grounds of a 'good try'.

The last swaggie just stood there looking nervous, and when St Peter looked beyond him to the doorway to Hell he quickly reached into his swag and pulled out a rather dirty pair of black lace lady's knickers and then handed them to the great saint.

'It's not much, but it is from Christmas,' said the swagman, coughing.

St Peter wasn't amused and only relented when the sundowner added: 'They're Carol's!'

SCAM!

The Irishman arrived at the Pearly Gates and confronted St Peter with a snarl and an urgent: 'Let me in!'

St Peter looked at the man and explained the procedure that he must provide credentials about his life on Earth before admission.

'Well, my good man, I was an arsonist, a swindler and an extortionist extraordinaire!' declared the burly Irishman.

St Peter looked at the man in amazement, and in a ringing voice declared: 'Then you cannot enter here.'

The Irishman glared at the Gate Keeper and in an equally loud voice declared: 'I'm not! I'm giving you ten minutes to get out!'

BEER YARNS

THE Daily Telegraph

ABOUT PETER LALOR

Peter Lalor's Beer column for *The Daily Telegraph* reconciled his love of beer with the need to earn a wage. When he discovered that many of the column's readers had the gift of the gab, he decided to combine their tales with some of his own for your reading pleasure.

He wishes to thank everybody who contributed to this book but warns some that he has handed their stories on to the authorities. You know who you are, and you should be ashamed.

Peter's wife Sue did the hard yards coordinating the project and reminding Peter that he should try to stick to the English language. Children Harry and Lucy were no help at all, although they have greatly contributed to Peter and Sue's need for beer and humour.

These days Peter is a senior writer for *The Australian*.

CONTENTS

He was a wise man who invented beer.

Plato

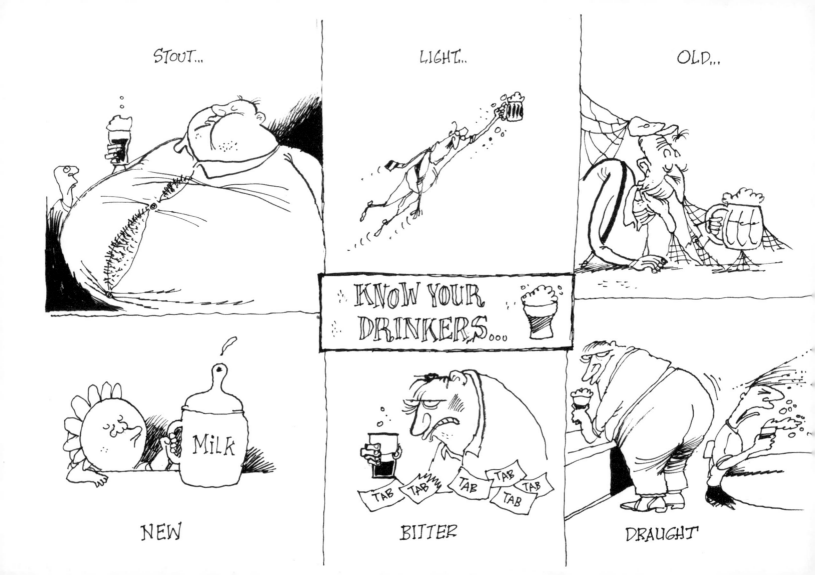

YARNS

A LONG WAY TO TIPPERARY

It was a hot day — a bloody hot day, in fact! We had been working the whole day on the mate's extensions — digging, levelling the dirt and mixing and pouring a tonne of concrete. Hot work. Thirsty work. It was getting late; the sun was well over the yardarm.

Mine host was a well-known tippler and so we had no fears that we would not be suitably rewarded for our sterling efforts on that day. Finally, it was time to down tools, stick our heads under the tap and hold out our hands in the time-honoured manner.

There is nothing like the expectation of an icy cold beer at the end of a long, hot day — and did we deserve it! (Has someone already said that?)

Our mate went to get the beers.

The minutes dragged on.

We'd heard the fridge open and close in the shed. What was he up to, slamming doors and that?

Then suddenly we heard curses, and the blue heeler, who'd been holed up in the cool of the shed, ran out yelping, followed by a cursing, spitting, red-faced bloke with murder in his eyes.

'Well, she's bloody done it this time!'

Dismayed, we listened and heard the sorry tale of last night's blue and his cringing appeasement that 'he really would give it up this time — no sweat'.

Of course, he didn't mean it, and had said the same thing many times, but nothing had ever come of it — who would take something like that seriously? The woman was obviously stark raving mad to empty a fridge full of grog on the one day when she knew he would need it and to replace it with bottles of water.

And to think we'd all said 'Bye' to her nicely when she drove off a few hours ago.

In a cupboard behind some motoring magazines he'd found a six-pack of fancy beer, left behind by some smarty at the big Hawaiian do we'd had a while ago (had a volcano at that one!). Even his teenage son — a chip off the old block if ever there was one — wouldn't come at it, so it had just sat there, gathering dust.

One of the blokes (he was a boy scout) chucked the water bottles onto the ground and shoved the six-pack into the remaining ice in the Esky, to take with us on the trip to the next house where, we were assured, there was a fridge full of grog just waiting for us.

Now, we are talking back in the bad old days here, when Sundays were as dry as a mother-in-law's kiss. The pubs were all shut.

Full of anticipation, we drove off chatting and laughing and hanging out for that cold one. We pulled up and strode confidently into his shed. He yanked the door open, talking over his shoulder to us, and I'll never forget his face when he saw the look on our faces as we saw inside. Shaking, he turned around and picked up the note from inside the empty fridge.

'She said you would come here. He needs help with his drinking, and so do you!'

A bit cheeky that, I thought.

So we piled back into the car and headed off to my place. The journey was made in grim silence. It was with a cold and sinking heart that I stopped in my drive. It was getting late by then and the house was shuttered and dark.

There was a faint glow from the shed at the back. We staggered like shipwrecked sailors towards the light.

She'd left the fridge door open and it wasn't until I'd wiped the tears from my eyes that I realised the note didn't say 'Up yours too' but 'You do too'.

Funny what a man's mind will do in extremis, isn't it?

Silently, Scout (we call him Scout now because of that night) went back to the car and handed us each a bottle of the foreign muck. The only word we could read on the label was 'Bier' and we had half an idea what that translated to.

We sat huddled in front of the open fridge, like worshippers of some ancient cargo cult, and sipped the semi-warm liquid. Had it been nectar of the gods, it would have been as ashes in our mouths.

But the last word goes to Baghdad (as in Baghdad — bombed all night).

'Well,' he said with a sigh. 'It certainly is a long way to Tipperary!'

Mike Sadler

A NEW EXPERIENCE

My future brother-in-law, who had recently arrived from Holland, and I went to the local hotel for a drink. I bought the first round of drinks and future brother-in-law then went to the bar for his shout.

He came back a short time later with two beers and said (with a strong Dutch accent), 'What is this beer? There is Old beer and . . .?'

I answered, 'New.'

He said, 'I wondered why the man laughed when I asked for two Young beers.'

Barry McKiernan

A THIEF'S HOBBY

The landlord of my local pub, Tom Collett MC, ex-RSM, Argyle and Sutherland Highlanders, was standing behind his lounge bar polishing glasses as he watched a lady customer surreptitiously sliding beer mats from the table into her handbag.

'Would Madam care to come to the bar? I will happily supply her with a complete selection of my beer mats rather than she clears them from the tables,' he called across the crowded bar.

The rather embarrassed lady made her way to the bar and stood before Tom, thanking him for being so kind.

'There must be a name for a collector of beer mats such as myself,' she said.

'There is, Madam,' Tom replied in a stern voice. 'A common bloody thief.'

Bernard Skitt

AUNT BERTHA'S CURE

In the 1950s, my favourite relatives were Aunt Bertha and Uncle Bill. They were a happy couple, but Aunt Bertha was bothered by Uncle Bill's beer drinking.

Every weekend he would bring home a sugar bag of bottled beer and have a binge. But Bill was a fit man and a happy drunk, always cracking a joke and slipping me (a ten year old) two bob.

Then someone showed Aunt Bertha this ad.

> *DRINK HABIT DESTROYED*
> *Thousands of homes ruined by drink have been made happy again by EUCRASY.*
> *All desire for alcohol is destroyed. Guaranteed harmless, tasteless, can be given secretly or voluntarily.*
> *State which wanted.*
> *Full twenty days' course 30/-*
> *DEPT. A, EUCRASY CO.*
> *297 Elizabeth St., Sydney*

She sent for this Eucrasy and when it arrived started putting it in his beer.

Like a lamb to the slaughter, he noticed no difference, but soon we all started to notice a difference in Uncle Bill. His hair started to fall out, he lost weight, he became morose. The doctors said he had stomach ulcers. Sadly, he died twelve months later.

People said, 'That's what the drink does to you,' but those of us in the know, knew it wasn't the beer but what was being put in it!

Heartbroken, lost, guilty — who knows? — Aunt Bertha died six months later.

Marcia Carr

I feel sorry for people who don't drink.
They wake up in the morning and that's the best
they're going to feel all day.

Dean Martin

BALLARAT BERTIE

About sixteen years ago a friend returned from Ballarat with a couple of bottles of CUB's Ballarat Bitter featuring Ballarat Bertie on the label. By this stage I was becoming well known for my willingness to try different beers. After sampling a bottle with some workmates the question was asked, 'How do we obtain some of this stuff, short of going to Ballarat?'

Taking up the challenge I phoned the local CUB depot at Cardiff. The reply was negative at best. 'No market for that stuff here and you have no liquor licence so we can't get it for you. You'll have to order it from Ballarat yourself.'

Undaunted, I consulted the Ballarat phone book and jotted down a few numbers. Ballarat Cellars was the first I rang and it proved positive. 'No worries,' said the proprietor, 'I'll send you ten cases and I'll look after the transport this end.'

The beer duly arrived, the cost being shared by the number who were prepared to try the Ballarat drop.

Blokes being blokes, quite a number of bottles were shared by those who ordered it. The initial curiosity about this unfamiliar product was prompted by the Ballarat Bertie label, but the creamy smooth taste of the product produced more than a favourable reaction.

In about two months pressure mounted for another order, this time for twenty cases. Ballarat Cellars again delivered the goods.

In one quality control session the question was asked, 'How about ordering a pallet? How do you think that would go?'

I replied, 'No problem, as long as we have most of the money up front. By the way, how many cases in a pallet?'

I found out it was sixty-four.

I started to mobilise the order. With a firm commitment to fifty cases I ordered the pallet. Thus began a more serious association between my group and Ballarat Cellars which was to last for quite a number of years until CUB stopped making Ballarat Bitter.

I would like to think that our orders had an impact on CUB making Ballarat Bitter for as long as it did.

Shortly after the initial pallet order it was extended to two pallets which became the standard order, except for Christmas when we ordered three pallets.

The unloading of the beer truck was quite a social event. A group of blokes would converge on my house about twenty minutes before the scheduled arrival of the truck. It's amazing how quickly a job can be accomplished when the workers have a common motivation.

I can only guess at the number of people who obtained Ballarat Bitter as a result of my orders. As I mobilised the larger order each person in turn could mobilise their own order of five to ten cases.

As I mentioned, the Ballarat Bitter deliveries became a great social focus; they also gave a reason to keep in touch with former work colleagues and to broaden the network of friends. For at least five people Ballarat Bitter was the only beer they purchased. Often the initiative for an order would come from members of the group itself and not from me.

Two pallets of Ballarat Bitter, 128 cases each containing one dozen long necks, carefully stacked and arranged in a suburban garage is an impressive sight, but alas, that is the past!

More recently a group of five people formed the Adamstown Heights Gentlemen's Club. It was formed at the suggestion of a friend and comprises three lower-middle-aged adult males and two young blokes in their early twenties.

The aims of the Gentlemen's Club are to enjoy each other's company whilst expanding one's knowledge of beer in order to appreciate the range of different tastes and styles.

At each meeting a member takes it in turn to invite a 'special guest' and tastings are held on a special themes basis. Themes to date include: Australia, Germany, United Kingdom, North America, Asia/Pacific, General Europe, Belgium . . . Bertie, look what you started!

Ed Tonks

BANK INSPECTOR

When a bank inspector called on a small country branch for a surprise audit he found the banking chamber deserted and the staff drinking beer in the manager's office. To teach them a lesson, he crept behind the counter and set off the hold-up alarm.

Much to his surprise, a barman from the pub next door immediately came running into the bank bearing a tray of fresh beers!

Bill Jones

BANNED FROM THE WOODYARD

Harry M was your classic old-school publican. His mother was a publican, his wife was, his father-in-law was and by now his son, Spud, is probably following in the old man's footsteps.

You may have seen Harry; for a brief time back in the 1960s he was Australia's own Marlboro man. And so you'd have thought Harry would have had more sympathy for a thirsty horse.

One of the first family pubs Harry ran was Melbourne's Lord Newry (coincidentally, the Lord Newry in question was an equerry to the Queen or somebody like that) at the bottom of Brunswick Street in North Fitzroy.

It was a working-class suburb in those days and the Newry had an honest working-class clientele consisting of bank robbers, SP bookies, assorted ex-cons and the odd bloke who pulled a wage. Okay, maybe the latter outweighed the former but it was a colourful place, at least until the trendies moved in.

Anyway, it was a pretty busy pub, especially on a Saturday when Fitzroy (now the Brisbane Bears) were playing at home. The oval was about 100 metres from the pub and at half-time a desperate pack of footy fans would flock to the bar where 7oz glasses were filled at an astonishing rate by bar staff armed with the sheep-drench-type guns that were fitted to the end of a hose and allowed them to fill a glass anywhere within about two metres — or squirt anyone obnoxious within five metres.

One group of Harry's regulars were the guys from the woodyard on the other side of the footy ground.

These blokes could get a bit rowdy at times and occasionally a bit silly. One day the boss of the yard had the delivery horse out the front of the pub and decided he'd bring it in for a drink.

Despite earning a quid on the back of the Marlboro horse, Harry couldn't see the funny side of this and promptly barred the woodyard boss, who we'll call Joe.

Now, it can get pretty cold down in Melbourne in winter and the pub of course got its wood from you know who.

When the first chill winds blew down Brunswick Street, Harry sent the barman down the road to buy some wood, but he came back empty-handed. Harry decided to go and see Joe who told him to f——k off out of his yard because he was barred.

For decades to come Harry would tell the yarn and boast that while he's met many a man who has been barred from a pub, he's never met another who was barred from a woodyard.

Peter Lalor

BEER AND MARRIAGE

In 1995, I was living by myself and I saw a cooking program on television. They were making 'Fish and chips with a twist'. The 'twist' was adding a can of your favourite chilled beer to the batter. They also showed you how to make the side salad.

After watching the program and taking note of the recipe, I went to buy the ingredients at my local supermarket. I collected all the necessary ingredients and placed them on the check-out counter. I then noticed that the person in front of me had the same kind of ingredients: flour, eggs, vegetable oil, tomatoes, baby spinach, Spanish onions and a deli parcel wrapped in white paper. Surely it wasn't fish?

It was uncanny, bizarre, and it couldn't possibly have been the same recipe. That's what I was telling myself anyway, hoping that no one else would notice.

How embarrassing.

I had a quick glance at the lady in front of me and just smiled. I don't think she knew what was happening. I finally paid for my groceries and left the supermarket in a hurry.

I was still missing one ingredient — the beer — so I entered the local bottle shop, grabbed a can from the fridge and went to the counter.

Lo and behold, I saw the same lady with the same beer as was used on the television program. It was also the same as the one I had in my hand.

My suspicions were confirmed.

She was quite attractive and me being a bloke, I couldn't let the opportunity pass by. I started a conversation with her and found out that she also saw the TV program and yep, she was cooking for her parents that night.

Somehow I managed to ask her out and eight months later we got married. Every year since, we have celebrated our anniversary with 'Fish and chips with a twist'.

Winston Lau

BEER AND SKITTLES

I would like to pass on a story that makes me laugh whenever I rekindle thoughts of that silly Sunday years ago.

It was out in the Central West of New South Wales and a few of us locals called into the Royal Hotel on a quiet Sunday afternoon. There were only about eight of us in the pub and we all settled back for a bit of a drink.

Later in the evening, with more than enough schooners aboard, a water cum beer fight erupted in the bar. The publican at the time, Frank W, couldn't keep out of a good fight so he hooked a hose to one of the beer lines and proceeded to spray down anyone who moved. Before you knew it we were sliding around in four inches of beer and water on the old lino floor.

The game we invented that day involved sliding along the length of the bar on your stomach with a bike helmet attached and hitting five 'skittles' with your head, the 'skittles' being two kegs placed on top of another three kegs.

Surprisingly, no one was hurt, but a few headaches were around the next day.

We found out later that Frank had to dispose of this lake of beer from his floor before his wife arose the next day.

We always thought Frank was a bit of a genius — he just drilled holes in the floor and drained the beer into the cellar.

Chris Dwyer

BEER DRENCH

A beer memory that springs to mind happened at one of our teenage parties held at home near Coonabarabran in the late 1960s. My father was a real wag as well as a good beer drinker, and was always thinking up tricks to play on us and our friends.

After an afternoon of playing tennis, eating and drinking, Dad appeared with a drench pack (a backpack normally filled with drench for sheep, cows, etc., that you squirted into the animal's mouth with a drench gun) on his back, full of beer. He proceeded to go around and drench our friends — if you wouldn't have the offered 'drench' orally, you ended up being squirted with beer.

Dad thought it was a huge joke, until the next morning when we got him with stale beer with the drench gun as he was waking up. Mum was not amused!

Penny Turner

BLACK DAYS

As a nipper (I was only sixteen) on the railways I used to go to the local pub — in fact the only pub — in the small town of Einasleigh in North Queensland with my two carpenter mates for a couple of beers while the camp oven stew was cooking. Our camp was only 200 yards out the back door of the pub by the railway siding.

On occasions there were Aboriginal stockmen or ringers out the back of the pub waiting for a ride back to the cattle station. This was back in the 1950s and publicans weren't allowed to sell beer or spirits to Aborigines, but some publicans would serve them drip tray beer — this was the stuff that spilt in the pour and was caught in the tray. The law soon cracked down on that and made sure the outback pubs put Condy's crystals in the drip tray and only sold beer in clear bottles. The rules were meant to put an end to the practice.

So this day Jimmy Carpentaria, an Aboriginal stockman from Carpentaria Station (they always took the name of the station as their surnames) asked me if I would bring out a bottle of 6d beer.

'Don't get the brown stuff,' he said. 'It tastes awful. Get me the purple beer. Better taste.'

Barry Williams

BORN IN A PUB

The following is true as far as I have been informed; I personally cannot remember.

I was born on the 15th of April 1933 at the Mount Lachlan Hotel, corner of Elizabeth and Raglan Streets, Waterloo, Sydney.

Washed and clothed, my proud father Jim presented me to the local clientele from behind the bar.

As the tale goes, one inebriated gentleman promptly placed his forefinger in his glass of beer and then into my mouth.

Thus my first taste of beer, less than one hour old.

Furthermore, I still enjoy it!

Kevin Hole

CAR WENT THE OLD WAY HOME

There's an old Sunday newspaper editor who, like many in his trade, was fond of keeping the ink in his blood balanced with booze. Now Fozzie, as we'll call him, was prone to all-night sessions and tended to get rather muddled.

One night he headed home before sunrise and was obviously sober enough to find his car. (These were the days when that was proof enough of your ability to drive.)

Anyway, Fozzie got home safely enough, parked the car in the driveway, somehow made his way inside and upstairs to bed beside his dearly beloved and promptly began to snore away like he hadn't a trouble in the world.

At least, that's the way he tells it.

Early next morning he rolled over, almost killing his wife with his beery breath, opened one bloodshot eye and thought, 'Hang on a minute . . . something's not right here.'

Poor Fozzie had woken up next to his first wife and somewhere in an adjacent suburb the second one was waiting in a very cranky mood.

'Bloody car went the old way home,' he told us later.

We believed him, but we're not sure if wife number two did.

Peter Lalor

COUNTING SHEEP

There's a story in our family about Dad not being able to sleep. He would lie there at night, tossing and turning. Mum suggested counting sheep, but that didn't work. In frustration she said, 'If you can't sleep and you can't count sheep try counting glasses of beer; that should come naturally to you.'

A few seconds passed and Dad got out of bed.

'Where are you going?' asked Mum.

'To get my first beer,' said Dad.

Chris Horneman

CROCKET

Crocket was the town character and regular at the Pioneer Hotel in the one-pub town of Boomi, northwest New South Wales.

It was noon on a November day in 1965 and a howling drought was in progress when a commercial traveller pulled up outside the hotel. He shook the dust off him and walked into the public bar where Crocket was sitting on a bar stool in the corner of the room.

The barmaid had just gone to the ladies room and the traveller waited impatiently for service, banging a two-shilling coin on the counter.

After a short while he turned to Crocket and said, 'How long has this town been dead for, mate?'

Crocket replied, 'Not long, mate; you're the first vulture to arrive.'

Peter Stehr

CURLY

When I was a teenager in the 1960s, it was the 'in' thing to set our hair in rollers using beer as a setting agent. Amazingly, it worked. Our curls lasted all day.

Pity about the smell.

Carole Smith

DRINK RIDER

I belong to an organisation that recreates the battles of the English Civil Wars of 1642–1660. At one of the weekends in St Albans the founder of the organisation, the Brigadier, was riding his horse from pub to pub in full seventeenth-century battle gear and accepting drinks from members. After about two hours of this he was approached by the police and told to dismount, as he was drunk.

After about fifteen minutes he mounted up and rode off to the pubs again. A police car pulled up and the police arrested the 'Brig' and charged him with being drunk in charge of a horse. At court he was convicted and fined.

Neil Chippendale

ERNIE

The Lord Newry regulars certainly had some history about them. One was an old bloke called Ernie, who by the time I got to know him looked like Billy McMahon's grandfather. Ernie was in his nineties and had big eyes and two enormous ears which must have continued to grow after the rest of him had started to shrink.

Ernie was so old he'd been a hansom cab driver in Brunswick Street as a lad.

Ernie loved a beer and would pop in most days as the Newry was early on his list of chores for the day.

Ernie was a busy man who knew almost everyone in Fitzroy and North Fitzroy and was always keen to catch up with every one of them at their individual pubs.

One day he was particularly downbeat when he dropped in for his first beer and told me that his best mate up at one of the other pubs had passed away, which left a bit of a hole in Ernie's routine. But, not for long.

When the bloke's will was read the relatives were horrified to find he had left an undisclosed sum in the care of the publican of his favourite pub and it was to be used to buy Ernie his beer every day.

Ernie was delighted and would check in each day and enjoy a shout from a dead mate.

Peter Lalor

FALSE TEETH

Old Mick had been drinking at his local pub for as long as anyone could remember and this day a young bloke came in and noticed that every time old Mick went to the toilet he would leave his false teeth in his beer.

Curiosity got the better of the young bloke so over he went and asked why.

Old Mick replied, 'I went to the toilet once and when I came back half me beer was missing, so in go the teeth and for some reason it doesn't happen any more.'

Garry Phipps

FLY IN BEER

In the good old days, around the early 1950s, I was living in Young, New South Wales. My late husband grew up in the area, but I had lived in Sydney all my life before moving there. We had two young children and not much money and I decided to earn a bit of extra cash one Sunday by cherry picking.

Leaving the two kids behind with a relative we set sail for the orchard which had advertised for cherry pickers. It was hard work for a city girl like me, but I was enjoying it.

About 10 a.m. the orchard owner's wife came out with freshly made scones and cakes and large pots of tea for our morning tea break.

One old-timer, a typical Aussie, got his tea and a fly fell into it.

'I'll have to throw that one out,' he said. 'You never know what germs they carry.'

Later that afternoon the same kind lady came out with some beer for all who wanted it and you would not believe it — the same old-timer got his beer, put it on the bench for a minute and a fly fell into it.

He got it out with his dirty finger and said, 'You can't waste a good beer,' and promptly drank it.

This is a true story and I've never been able to work out how he could not drink his tea, but the beer was okay.

Mrs E Shelley

HEAD BANGER

I was enjoying my second pint of Canberra Pride with the then Master Brewer for the Wig & Pen pub, Richard Pass. Richard was explaining the palate qualities of a higher temperature, slightly hopped, slightly malty ale and, being dedicated to the enjoyment of all things brown, dark brown and black, I was into it.

In keeping with this tour and with my palate being challenged at every mouthful, Richard suggested a change to an effervescent cold Kiandra Gold.

This was really hitting the spot, and two of these — followed by explanations and tasting of the wonderful Ballyragget Red — had me slightly infected but raring to go.

Richard's next choice, the intriguingly named but superb tasting Aviator Bock, had me asking for detailed recipes and further explanation regarding its naming. I must confess that by now Richard was slightly infected himself.

With some mirth he announced the following: 'Bock is a high alcohol content dark beer enjoyed by German landowners and the like and one should look out for one's self when consuming more than the one or two. In fact, true to its name, "Bock" is the last thing you will hear as your head hits the tiles on the pub floor!'

So endeth the tour and the lesson.

Paul Cairns

You're not drunk if you can lie on the floor without holding on.

Joe E Lewis

HORSE-PITELL-ITY

Many years ago on the kind of stinking hot evening that only Sydney can turn on, I took a visiting Scottish friend down to the Quay for a ferry ride.

Sydney left him speechless.

'What,' I asked cockily, 'is it that you particularly like about our city?'

'Och aye, it's yer horse-pitell-ity, no doubt abert-it.'

We had moved to a seat close to the berthing ferry when I noticed someone had left a brown paper bag there. In it were two very cold, very large bottles of beer.

'Yes,' I said, not missing a beat and reaching for the trusty bottle opener I carried back then. 'It even extends to this arrangement for leaving a couple of coldies around the traps for parched blow-ins from Scotland.'

Glug-glug-glug . . . we each took a few healthy swigs.

I smiled at him confidentially. 'You're lucky, you know, mate; you're drinking a Reschs Dirty Annie.'

He frowned a little, then quickly put the bottle to his mouth and drained it.

'Aye, it's yer horse-pitell-ity!' was all he could say.

Lloyd O'Brien

HOW'S ABOUT A KISS?

As an avid armchair gardener, his nose attracted me at once. In my time I have judged Italian tomatoes and early lettuce and was once co-opted onto a sub-committee to discuss the merits of a particularly fine King Edward potato. His nose, had it been in a different position, could well have won a prize in the red onion section of the local horticultural show.

After that, the rest of his face was something of a disappointment. There were hints of glorious purple in the broken veins that littered his cheeks like motorway intersections and the puce of his ears matched a popular shade of lipstick in an economy range. But the foundation was a common, agricultural ruddiness that can only have come from life out-of-doors.

I rather pride myself on my complexion. I inherited it from my mother. When she died at eighty-three after a blameless life led entirely without recourse to artificial face creams, the undertaker in an undertone remarked that she had one of the finest skins he had seen during forty years in the trade.

Recollected gems like that can enrich many a winter morning. I admit that I do use 'Bliss' just to keep the wrinkles at bay; I believe I owe it to my friends. Of course, one's diet is so important, too. Rich foods I avoid like the plague and alcohol I take only in moderation.

However, that particular evening was an exception. I really could have killed for a glass of beer. I had just spent a frightful four hours driving in pouring rain on an outback track that more closely resembled the Limpopo River mudflats than a vehicular thoroughfare. Only the absence of hippopotami persuaded me that I was still in Australia.

I found the hotel quite by chance; in the gathering dusk its welcoming lights presaged a life-saving oasis. It stood in splendid isolation as a memorial to a short-lived copper-mining boom in the 1890s and it was clear that precious little had been spent on it since.

A Trappist monk would have felt at home in my cell-like bedroom, while anyone lucky enough to find the bathroom could have been inspired to write a treatise on the history of plumbing. I moved closer to the bar with the hesitant anticipation of an occasional drinker trespassing on private ground.

He was the only occupant of the Public Bar. He squinted at me from beneath bushy eyebrows that sprouted haphazardly like the whiskers of a mature walrus. His greasy, greying hair receded from a furrowed forehead and cascaded untidily into a ponytail.

The fragrance of his pomade was intriguing and not one with which I was familiar; a member of the Salvation Army might have recognised it. I use 'Sensation'; in an instant it suggests masculinity without the obtrusive biceps, and culture without an overtly gay label. I have also found that a little 'Power' on the cheeks after shaving encourages women to be more attentive. It hints at hidden wealth without fostering undue extravagance.

His clothing was what I would describe as bush or weekend Australian. He wore a T-shirt that stretched optimistically but not entirely successfully over a sagging stomach. It clearly had only a nodding acquaintance with the laundrette and I could not possibly repeat its illustrated caption in mixed company.

The pungency of his sun-dried sweat reminded me of Moroccan camel dung; not entirely unpleasant in the thin night air at a Berber encampment on the edge of the Sahara Desert but somewhat overpowering within the confines of a Public Bar. The leather belt supporting his jeans was only narrowly winning the battle of decency. His muddy sneakers added to the unwashed aura that surrounded him.

Although sartorial elegance is not a noticeable feature of the Australian outback, I believe my outfit on that occasion would have found favour with my tailor. After a long bath liberally dosed with essential oils, I chose neutral colours. My silk tie, reminiscent of ripening corn, accompanied a cream shirt and a fetching sleeveless pullover in Nile Sand that my Aunt Edith had given me at my request the Christmas before. My cotton trousers were Inca Stone, a popular choice in London that year, while pale tangerine socks contrasted rather well with shoes in a nice shade of African native brown. (There, I have remembered not to use that other word.)

He said nothing, but gazed pensively into his empty glass as I approached the bar. I detected stale tobacco smoke and instinctively looked for his nicotine-stained fingers and matching teeth to confirm his addiction to the weed.

I am not an intolerant man but I do dislike tobacco smoke. It assaults my senses and permeates my clothing; it lingers like a malevolent spirit, abroad long after it should have been laid to rest. I sniffed the air sensitively in much the same way that a prairie dog assesses imminent danger in the Arizona desert; against all odds, my craving for beer kept me moving forward.

As I stood at the bar I inclined my head towards him. Experience has taught me that presenting a friendly disposition to the natives does no harm, however unsavoury strange bars may be. However, in my opinion, too much familiarity breeds contempt and should be avoided at all costs.

I believe that an Englishman's self-sufficiency in foreign lands can be traced back to the Norman Conquest and the conquerors' penchant for constructing castles; I plan to write a monograph on the subject on my return to England.

He did not return my glance at first. In the light of subsequent events, he may have been shy or perhaps just suffering from the early stages of dipsomania. A slight twitch of the hand holding his empty glass did suggest that drink was uppermost in his mind.

The first words he uttered were indistinct. They sounded like 'Pommy bastard'. He might have said 'Tommy Custard', although that's not my name.

Perhaps Tommy was the barman.

The next words were clearer. 'Have a beer, mate.' My moment had arrived. I beamed at him in a manner calculated to put him at his ease. 'That's very kind of you,' I said as I sat down on a bar stool beside him. 'I'll have a Four Kisses please.'

I think he misunderstood me. With an agility that surprised me and would probably have alarmed his doctor, he reached the exit in ten seconds flat.

As the door swung shut, his parting words echoed like thunder across the bar. 'Pommy bastard' was clearer this time but I was unable to recognise everything that followed.

The barman later told me that he had never before heard such a fine range of Australian expletives expressed in such a short space of time. I consider myself fortunate to have been present.

James Hamilton

HUMPTY DUMMIES

While I was travelling around Australia with a mate we stumbled across a pub in Humpty Doo in the Northern Territory. With the locals just being their bizarre selves, we decided to sit for a while.

We got talking and drinking cold ales from the tap after a great but stinking hot day, when the locals told us that the fishing club was having a do on that night.

We stayed, but at the end of the night had to drive two kilometres to a camping spot for the night. There was a policeman outside the pub waiting for the first person to take off for home as everyone in the pub was drunk (and driving).

One person in the pub was not drinking so I suggested that he walk outside, pretend to stumble to his car, and drive off very quickly in the opposite direction to which most of us were going.

He took off in his car. The policeman gave chase and everybody piled out into their cars and straight home. Everyone got home alive, well, and without coming across the constabulary.

One of the funniest sights was watching all the people run for their cars as if there was a breakout at the prison.

We called back the next day and they were still laughing; I think they were still drunk too.

Paul Staunton

I SAW THE LIGHT

One Friday night in 1983 I'd had a long session at the Drummoyne Rowing Club. Then one of my mates asked me if I wanted to go with them to Vaucluse. I figured they were going to a party so I said yes.

There were four of us in the car, but one bailed at Double Bay because the driver was a maniac.

When we got to Vaucluse my mate (no names) in the front of the car got out and I figured he was just checking out how the party was. After a while I asked the driver why he was taking so long and his answer led me to believe that the guy was doing a break and enter.

Now, I wasn't so keen to hang around, but in my condition I wasn't able to go too far. It was a very windy night and with all the beer I'd drunk I soon needed to go for a piss. The only place I could see that would give me shelter was a house under construction down the street at a T intersection.

After I'd had a leak I stepped up from the clay in the front of the yard and saw searchlights in the sky and straight away thought that the police helicopter had been called in to search for my mate.

I couldn't hear the helicopter because there was a gale blowing, but it was hanging around so I went back to the house and waited. I kept checking, but the helicopter was still there and I was too scared to go back to the car in case I was seen.

Next thing I knew I woke up with floorboards inches from my face . . . I'd fallen asleep under the house. It's amazing where you can sleep after a few beers. Anyway, I climbed out from under the house, covered in clay and trying to remember what had happened the previous night.

As I stepped up onto the footpath and lit a cigarette it all started to come back. Then I looked up to where I'd seen the helicopter, feeling relieved I hadn't been caught up in the mess, only to find I was looking at the South Head lighthouse!

Bruce Dowling

IT AIN'T HEAVY . . .

My wife and I were invited to my sister's home for Christmas dinner.

My brother-in-law Len is a keen beer lover and for Christmas we had bought him a 24-bottle case of 'Celebrate the Millennium' Crown Lager.

I had planned to drive from our home on the Central Coast to Lorraine and Len's place at Jannali, but my wife, knowing that I like a celebratory drink myself, insisted we travel by train for safety.

I had to lug the heavy case of beer over two kilometres to our nearest railway station, sit it on my lap for safekeeping on the one and a half hour journey to Central Station, carry it again for what seemed like miles to the train platform for services to Jannali, and hold on to it for the forty-minute journey to Jannali and then walk from the station, finishing with the climb up a steep hill to our destination.

To ease the burden I sang a song on the way: 'It ain't heavy (well, it was, but you know what I mean), it's for my brother.'

I was so relieved when I touched down at my sister's, and just found enough strength to grab my first coldie for Chrissie.

Len was overjoyed with this thoughtful gift, which made the effort worth the while.

Imagine my surprise upon opening my Christmas present from Lorraine and Len to find — you guessed it — a 24-bottle case of 'Celebrate the Millennium' Crown Lager.

Of course, I took it home with me on our long return journey. There was no way I was going to leave 'my' carton with beer-loving Len.

Martin New

The problem with some people is that when they aren't drunk, they're sober.

William Butler Yeats

STUBBIES

THROWDOWNS...

MOLOTOV COCKTAIL...

Petrol

KNOW YOUR BEER BOTTLES...

24 x 375 ml
24 x 375 ml
VB

SLAB...

LONGNECKS

DEAD MARINE

MEDICINAL PURPOSES

In the late 1980s my family owned a small holiday home on the northern Central Coast of New South Wales. Situated in an ideal location close to the beach, lake and local watering hole, it was the venue for many memorable weekends shared amongst a large circle of friends aged in their mid twenties. We would regularly travel from our homes in northern Sydney on a Friday evening to spend our leisure hours surfing, fishing and of course partaking of the odd ale.

As one particular weekend approached the usual sojourn was planned. On the Thursday before, I was approached by a friend named Mark who was overjoyed at having a half work day on Friday; he asked if he could have the house keys to travel up early with another friend to get a head start on the weekend. Mark was a trusted friend; therefore I could see no reason to deny this request. Arrangements were made for him to pick up the keys from our house at lunchtime on Friday.

The following day Mark arrived on time, perched upon his preferred mode of transport — the beloved Suzuki 750cc motorcycle. Surprisingly, another friend, Chris, who at the time was unemployed, had made a spur of the moment decision to travel with Mark as a pillion passenger. They were leaving early to enjoy the fine weather, and spent a short time with my mother before heading off with sleeping bags and luggage attached to the rear of the cycle.

I arrived home around 3 p.m., and within an hour was joined by the others who intended travelling that afternoon. Just prior to our departure I received a phone call from Chris. They had come off Mark's motorcycle on the F3 Freeway, and he had been transported to Hornsby Hospital by ambulance with some minor leg injuries. Mark's whereabouts were unaccounted for; however, Chris assured me he was not badly injured. Despite our concerns, Chris assured us he was okay and would soon be discharged into his mother's care (she was already there).

I made a few phone calls, but in those days before the mobile phone if someone wasn't home it was anyone's guess as to what they were up to. I did establish, however, that Mark was not taken to hospital. So with that unexpected delay we commenced the hour-long journey north.

On the way the conversation centred on Mark. What had happened? How was he? Where was he? We need not have worried, for our minds were soon to be put at ease. As we neared the holiday house I saw the blinds were parted and the wooden front door clearly open behind the mesh door. Our convoy of vehicles stopped out the front and the group slowly congregated outside the front door. Someone was certainly home. Most of us assumed that Mark had somehow managed to continue his journey.

However, several hard knocks on the door failed to draw any response. We circled round the back through the old steel gate and as the rear yard came into view I saw a sight I will never forget.

Mark had managed to ride his somewhat worse for wear motorcycle to the house and park it in the rear yard. He had then grabbed a full carton of cold beer stubbies and a beanbag from the house. He had placed the beanbag in the middle of the back yard, cut the bottom out of the beer carton, exposing the base of the stubby bottles, then placed the carton upside down in the bean bag. He had then positioned his red raw rump, complete with gravel rash and lacerations, squarely in the centre of the beer in an attempt to alleviate the pain of the road rash he suffered in the accident. His shredded and bloody jeans were draped across the crashed motorcycle.

So there he was, sunning himself in the middle of the yard with his bum on a slab. He looked at us and said, 'See, guys, I told you the beer is strictly for medicinal purposes.'

The rest of the weekend was just as interesting, but this memory is priceless and permanently etched in my mind.

Glenn Gilbert

MY UNCLE

My favourite beer story concerns my cousin's wedding, which occurred in April 1955 when bottled beer was very scarce.

Having frequented the local pub for the major part of his working life, my uncle was able to talk the publican into parting with a few bottles of the precious liquid.

The future groom, with the help of his intended father-in-law, ended up with ten dozen large bottles which they stored under the uncle's bed. A very safe place to keep it, for the wedding was only two weeks away.

Although not yet retired from work, my uncle took a few days off to get things ready for the wedding.

The beer was purchased on Tuesday; the following Monday my uncle came out in the morning complaining of being a bit crook. 'And rightly so,' said his daughter. 'You should be dead, you bastard; you've drunk all the grog.'

Upon investigation the ten dozen were ten dozen empty bottles as well as three whisky, one brandy and one Pimms bottle. Fair enough, a good drink for a little under a week; however, he still managed to carry out his regular sessions at the local every day.

The same uncle came home after a big session with his mate and realised he had no keys to get inside. After a lot of discussion, they decided to get in through the laundry window. Using a ladder from under the house, and after much difficulty, the window was opened and uncle slid in, into a tub full of soaking washing. Naturally, when they came to open the door they found that it had not been locked.

My uncle's drinking bouts are a legend in an unbelievable family history.

Terry Hayes

OUCH

We were holidaying on the Central Coast several years ago. Dad was planning a big Australia Day party and had been buying stacks of beer which was all stored in an old fridge on the verandah of the two-storey house where we were staying.

Mum and Dad were staying overnight in Sydney and my sister and I were alone in this strange house. We heard a car pull up nearby and, spying through the blinds, we saw two youths heading for the house, apparently up to no good.

Downstairs was well locked but upstairs the verandah area was quite open. To our horror one of them started to climb the tall timber pole leading to the verandah.

'They're after Dad's beer,' we whispered.

'Never!' we agreed.

I told my sister to ring 000 and to ring Dad while I grabbed some cold tinnies and started throwing them at the invader. I'm a netball player and I didn't miss with many.

The climber was taking a battering but still seemed to be coming up.

We knew the police were a long way away and would take ages to get there and the other thief had started to climb up the other pole.

We were just about to give up the attack and retreat to the bedroom, which had sturdy locks, when we heard a siren. No, not the police, it was an ambulance coming to the would-be thieves' rescue.

Apparently, in her panic my sister had been giving the operator a blow by blow description. 'Ooh! She's hit him on the head . . . Ooh! She's hit him again!'

The woman thought the intruders needed an ambulance more than we needed the police.

Fortunately the siren's noise was enough to scare the robbers and they took off.

We saved Dad's beer.

Dad said we deserved a medal, but we settled for a trip to Surfers.

Oh, the party was a great success and probably resulted in a few more sore heads.

Louise Carr

IN CASE OF FIRE

VICTORIA VB BITTER

WARREN

PRAISE GOD AND PASS THE VB

Here is my favourite beer story. It sounds like a tall tale, but I can assure you that every word is true, because it happened to me.

I had just come out from a church meeting and was attempting to start my car. No matter how hard I tried, I could not get the engine to come to life.

It seemed that it was out of petrol, so my pastor took me for a ride to the petrol station to fill up a tin. We came back and emptied the tin of fuel in the petrol tank and tried again, but still nothing.

By now we had three pastors and some friends surrounding the car.

Two friends of one of the men present were walking along the road, after having consumed several longnecks of VB. Each was carrying a bottle as they walked. They approached us and watched for a couple of minutes while we poured some petrol in the carburettor and tried to start the engine, still without luck. (It turned out later that the fuel line was blocked.)

Soon one of these two piped up and said that he had a solution. He downed the rest of his beer and poured some petrol into the bottle. He instructed me to keep turning the key and pressing the accelerator, while he continued to pour petrol from his bottle into the carburettor.

This seemed to give it some life for a few seconds, and then suddenly I saw a huge flash from where I sat in the car. The petrol had caught alight and this bloke was holding a 'Molotov cocktail'.

To make things worse, the engine bay had caught alight as the petrol spilt out of the bottle.

It was like an inferno. What happened next occurred over a couple of seconds, but it seemed like an eternity.

The spectators by now had moved a couple of metres away onto a driveway. This bloke with the blazing VB looked at the bottle, looked at me and looked back at the bottle. His eyes went wide and he lobbed the bottle up into the air, and bang, straight onto the driveway in the middle of the onlookers.

The driveway went up in flames while people went diving for cover. (No one was burnt, thank the Lord.)

Meanwhile, I was sitting in the driver's seat watching my engine bay go up in flames.

Quick as a flash, the other bloke ripped the twist top off his unopened longneck and proceeded to shake it vigorously. He then sprayed the golden drop into the engine bay and put the fire out. I couldn't believe it.

I know that if we'd had a video camera we would have won 'Australia's Funniest Home Videos' with this effort. One thing is for sure — I don't think I will ever again hear three pastors and a group of Christians declaring the virtues of VB so enthusiastically!!

David Keane

Reality is an illusion that occurs
due to lack of alcohol.

Anonymous

SCHOONER GRIP

A mate of mine once did a favour for a friend. When the job was finished the friend asked, 'How much do I owe you?'

'Don't worry about it; buy me a beer next time you're in the pub,' my mate replied.

A couple of weeks later the friend walked into the local, saw my mate and ordered an extra beer. He walked over to him and said, 'Here's that beer I owe you,' and handed it to him.

It promptly fell through my mate's outstretched hand and smashed on the pub floor.

'Why did you drop that beer?' the bloke asked.

'Because,' my mate replied patiently, 'this is a Schooner Grip not a Middy Grip.'

Needless to say he was bought schooners from then on and they fitted perfectly.

Garry Phipps

SINKING A BEER

This story goes back to the year 1935 when I was prospecting at a place called Southern Cross in the Western Australian goldfields.

Two old prospectors sank a shaft in the main street of the town, opposite the hotel, and spent as much time in the pub as working in the mine.

As the shaft got deeper the bloke operating the windlass would pop into the pub, come out with two foaming pots of beer and call out to his mate at the bottom of the shaft that 'a beer was coming down'. He would put a pot on top of the bucket attached to the cable of the windlass and ever so carefully lower the beer to his mate.

This procedure was repeated many times throughout the day.

I had the privilege of sharing a couple of beers with them on a few occasions and learned a lot from their experiences as prospectors and Drinkers of Beer.

Norm Woodcock

THAT COCKY'S DEAD

During the 1930s I met up with a couple of old prospectors in a pub at a place called Marvel Loch on the goldfields of Western Australia. After a few beers they told me they were about to have a few tons of gold-bearing quartz transported to the Government Battery for crushing.

To save them a few bob I offered to cart the ore in my T Model Ford (converted to a utility truck) to the Battery. The crushing yielded about 20 ounces of nugget gold worth about 100 quid.

These two old boys were very thankful for my help and insisted on repaying me, so off we went to a place called Southern Cross and booked into a boarding house for the night.

Next stop: the local pub for a 'few' beers.

Like all prospectors, these two guys could put away the beer. After a while I left them to it, went to the boarding house and had a feed, then went upstairs to an open verandah which contained three beds, one cage and one cockatoo.

My two friends returned several hours after, their arms laden with bottles of beer. They were up and down all night, drinking and urinating in the cocky's cage. The poor cocky would splutter and squawk every time they went to the cage, which was quite understandable.

And so it went on, until suddenly there was a squawk and an eerie silence.

I managed a little sleep but was up at dawn to see my two companions dead to the world. I looked in the cage and saw the poor bloody bird — stone dead on the bottom of the cage.

I still don't know to this day whether the cocky died of poisoning, drowning or a screwed neck — probably all three, I fancy.

I had those two blokes out of bed and into Tin Lizzie and off to Marvel Loch before they were awake.

I took sympathy on the old prospectors and dropped into a pub on the way back. Needless to say, I gave that boarding house a wide berth whenever in Southern Cross.

I met many prospectors on the goldfields and they were a great bunch of fellows. These two were no exception and I guess they are still prospecting up in the Great Beyond. I hope Saint Peter shouts them a beer now and then — and doesn't let them anywhere near the cockies.

Norm Woodcock

THE LOST BEERS

Many years ago my husband was organising a barbecue during the war years. He and his mates would buy schooners of beer and fill quart bottles, as take-away beer was as rare as hen's teeth.

They were going to Sans Souci near Mick Moylan's Hotel to have a barbecue on the beach.

My husband said he would keep the beer cold by burying it in the sand near the surf. After a while everything was ready so he went to get the beer, but couldn't find it as the tide had come in.

He had to outrun all his mates and hitch home.

Paulene Lowe

THERE IS A GOD

This is a true story. I went to a Catholic high school in the Manly Warringah area (St Augustine's College in Brookvale). When I was in Year Twelve, I had an Irish priest, Father Ward, a teacher of Religious Education.

As we were in our final year of school the class was fairly relaxed and Father Ward treated us with the respect that young adults deserve. I remember that during one of the classes someone asked Father Ward if he really believed in God and miracles.

We were fortunate enough to have the following story told to us as his way of replying to the question.

It was the middle of summer on a Sunday, one of those days when the temperature rose over forty degrees early in the afternoon. Father Ward had performed a Mass earlier that day and was trying to enjoy the rest of his Sunday as God had intended — putting his feet up and watching the cricket on the TV.

The heat was becoming unbearable and as the majority of ads on the TV between overs were beer commercials, he started to long for an ice cold beer. As a priest, he was on a weekly allowance of about $7 a week and as a smoker, he had already blown his allowance and did not have the money to nip down the road to the pub to buy a beer.

He looked to the heavens and prayed for a beer. A little while later there was a knock on the door. Father Ward arose from a heat-induced coma to see who it was. When he opened the door there was no one to be seen.

He looked down, and there sitting on the step was a six-pack of ice cold beer with a note attached.

He bent down and picked up the beer and read the note.

It was from a parishioner who had been in Mass that morning. The parishioner wanted to thank Father Ward for his moving sermon which had been a comfort to him and, it being such a hot day, he felt a cold beer was the best way of doing so.

Now, the priest's not sure if God had heard his plea for a beer, or if God had told the parishioner to deliver the beer, or if it was God who had inspired his sermon in Mass that morning. One thing he was sure of — he was thankful to God for the ice cold beer.

Mark Bressington

THIS ONE LOOKS ARMLESS

Like most Australian blokes Gordon L was prepared to go the extra yard for the institutions he held dearest. Now we're not talking surf clubs, scout groups or even local government. Gordon, like many of us, loved his local and would do anything for the boys and their home away from home.

After one heavy session Gordon and a mate were driving along a road about 100 kilometres south of Darwin when they saw a snake. It was clearly too early to have the DTs so the lads knew this crawling creepy was the real thing.

Remembering that the boys back at the pub dearly wanted a python for the fish tank — don't even ask what happened to the fish — Gordon decided to take matters in hand.

He stumbled out onto the road and with his best beer goggles on attempted to grab what was clearly a harmless boa constrictor.

Course it ish!

Well, almost harmless and almost a python; unfortunately, Gordon had set his muddled sights on a 2.8-metre deadly king brown snake with a head the size of a fist.

'I made the mistake of grabbing it with my left hand because I was holding a beer in my right,' he said later.

You can see from our intrepid bushman's comments that he was perhaps a little more devoted to his beer than his health and things were clearly going to get a little sticky.

'I had its head in my hand, but it got loose and grabbed the web of my left hand. Its fangs were that big it ripped my hand open,' Gordon said.

Still gripping the beer, he wrestled the snake into a sack, never spilling a drop in the process.

Gordon, like most of us who've woken with a hangover only to go back and fight the good fight next Friday night, was not a man who was once bitten twice shy. Angry, confused, and perhaps not thinking as clearly as he should have, he stuck his hand back in the bag.

Maybe he was making sure it really was a biting snake.

'I stuck my hand back in the bag and it must have smelled blood,' Gordon said. 'It bit me another eight times.'

Upset by the snake's hostility, Gordon withdrew and started to lose consciousness, but luckily for him he had a friend who cared.

'My mate was trying to keep me awake by whacking me in the head and pouring beer on me,' Gordon recalls.

His good friend decided to drive him to Darwin, but only got as far as the Noonamah Hotel, about fifty kilometres from the city, where the bar manager called an ambulance.

Sensible bloke that.

Gordon was in a coma for six weeks and had continuous blood transfusions because the venom prevented clotting and caused internal bleeding.

Up at the Darwin hospital they don't muck around and they decided to lop off the poor bloke's arm. His heart stopped three times during the amputation — probably shocked that it would be going through life with one less drinking apparatus.

The doctors said that Gordon was the sickest man ever to survive a snake bite, although you probably didn't need a medical degree to figure that out.

'I still can't believe my arm's been chopped off,' Gordon said later.

Gordon's sister reckoned her brother was accident-prone.

'He's like a cat, but this time he has used up his ninth life,' she said.

Gordon once spent three months in hospital after his car hit a buffalo and was crushed when a truck reversed and pinned him to a pile of bricks.

'I still have my life and I guess that's the most important thing,' Gordon said later.

Yeah, pal, but what about the bloody boys at the pub? What about the fish tank? Talk about self-centred!

Peter Lalor

WATER CLOSET

Back where I came from, a particular local businessman and his family were held in pretty high esteem. They were a nice enough family, but some of the older boys didn't quite live up to the high standards set by their mother and father.

One night the lads played up when the olds were out and got a little carried away. When the parents got home they noticed nothing wrong until they got out of the car and heard groaning from the garden bed by the driveway.

Dad got the torch and steering lock and approached the noise with some caution. Moving the torch around the ferns and what have you he couldn't help but notice a smell and then, to his horror, he found a near-naked man semi-conscious among the plants.

After some further investigation it was established that this rather drunk and bruised person was the number two son who had fallen from the balcony above while taking a leak.

Worse was in store.

The mother opened the door of the house to hear terrible cries from the bedroom of number three son, the youngest. Running in, she was passed by son number one who appeared to be sleepwalking in his underpants.

Inside number three's room was a terrible scene.

The sobbing little fella told Mum how his big brother had come barging in and without a word had opened the wardrobe, pulled out the sock drawer, urinated in it, pushed the drawer back in, closed the door and then left.

It seems the eldest had turned left instead of right and in his rather inebriated state had mistaken the kid's closet for a water closet.

Apparently this isn't an unusual thing, as I knew a bloke who mistook his turntable (remember them?) for the urinal. He'd wandered into the lounge room, lifted the lid and closed it again when finished — clearly a bloke under the thumb.

Peter Lalor

WATER POLICE, WARM FEET AND A BEER SHOWER

Back in the late 1950s I used to drink in a pub in Penshurst Street, Chatswood, called Ryans. Pretty tough pub too; bloodhouse they used to call it.

In this pub drank a bloke called Ole Sepp — great old bloke sober, but after three pints he thought he was superman.

Anyway, poor Old Sepp was always getting turfed out, usually spending the night in the local lockup.

This particular night he saw the police coming and took off out the door and jumped into the old horse trough that was still there and yelled, 'You can't touch me. This is a job for the water police.'

In those days — late 1950s, early 1960s — you could not get a drink on a Sunday unless you went to Windsor or Penrith (bonafide traveller, it was called).

Anyway, we used to have barbecues nearly every Saturday night ending late Sunday. One night all thirty of us flaked out round the large fire we had.

Next morning a mate called Monty woke up groaning, 'Geez, my feet.' He went to stand up and fell over. We rushed over to help him and when we removed his boots the bottoms of his feet fell off. It seems his feet had cooked through his boots as he was too near the fire. The poor bugger was in hospital for weeks and off work for months.

When we asked him what woke him up, he said, 'I got cold.'

Monty, the same bloke, was always tinkering with home-brew. The only trouble was, he could not stick to his recipe.

I remember one brew he put down; some clown told him to add raisins to it to give it a kick. He invited a half dozen of his mates to try it out. Bloody hell! Talk about dynamite! Bloody bottles blew up everywhere. Blokes had cut hands, cut faces — beer all over us.

When we finally got a few poured it tasted like Purple Para (the cheap plonk of the day) with a head on it. The bloody stuff was so dangerous we had to throw a blanket over the remaining bottles and were not game to go near it. I think Monty ended up throwing rocks at them to smash the damn things.

R T Noble

WATERING DOWN THE BEER

It was Christmas day 2000 in Ballina and we were very much anticipating the scrumptious lunch ahead of us. The day was hot and humid and what better way to start out than to have a nice cold drink? For my Mum and myself it was a glass of champers, for the boys a cold beer — Cane Toad beer, in fact! It came as part of a Christmas food hamper sent by my brother. From memory, the Cane Toad beer packed a punch at 7 per cent alcohol content.

In view of this fact, my Dad, not being too much of a seasoned drinker, like my husband Steve, decided to make his into a shandy. Steve had made a special trip down to the local shop to grab a bottle of lemonade. So Dad proceeded to dilute his Cane Toad beer with the lemonade.

Each time he took a swig he couldn't believe just 'how strong this bloody Cane Toad beer is', so much so that he went back to the fridge to get that bottle of lemonade about three times! What he really couldn't understand was why the beer wasn't getting a nice head — the more lemonade he added, the flatter it went. He thought that the strength of the alcohol must be causing the lemonade to go instantly flat!

It wasn't until Steve noticed that the bottle of lemonade he had bought hadn't yet been opened, that the 'penny dropped'. Dad had been using the bottle of cold water (incidentally, in a lemonade bottle) to 'water' his beer down! In the end a glass of champagne was in order while Steve enjoyed his full strength Cane Toad beer! On our return to Sydney, my brother asked how Dad had enjoyed the beer . . . Well, um . . .

Hillary Greenup

A tavern is a place
where madness is sold by the bottle.

Jonathan Swift

WATERING THE GARDEN

After a long night of good friends, good food and good beer, hubby, after saying his farewells as they drove away, 'took short'. As the little house was already occupied, he decided to water the flowers beneath the small rail-less balcony. He took one step too many, breaking his leg on the concrete surround.

On arrival, the ambulance officers asked how he fell. He promptly told them he had been pushed.

'Pushed by whom?' they asked.

'Hahn,' was the reply.

'Hahn who?' asked the ambulance officer.

'Hahn Ice,' he replied.

After a pin and plate inserted and six weeks in plaster I guess he'll watch where he waters next time (or how much he drinks).

Mary Smith

WRONG NUMBER

It was a much more innocent time. Christmas Eve, about 5 p.m., temperature hovering around 100 degrees. My mother, a devout and unquestioning Catholic, sat fanning herself on the front verandah.

The sound of our phone intruded on the heavy atmosphere.

'It's yerself, Mrs Shepherd?'

My mother recognised Father O'Dougherty's voice.

'Would yer be so good as ter send me around a half dozen of the usual cold ones as soon as yer can?'

My mother, although none too pleased, agreed.

'I think he drinks Sheaf Stout,' she said crossly, pulling me by one ear as I attempted to beat a hasty retreat, and reaching for her purse.

Soon I was staggering to the presbytery door.

'What's this lovely beer you've got here, Junie Benson?'

Father O'Dougherty was completely puzzled.

It turned out he thought he'd rung Shepherd's corner store for his weekly supply of Marchant's lemonade.

However, he did NOT insist I take the Sheaf Stout home and I've always believed it did not go to waste.

June Benson

FROTHY FACTS

BARMAID BANS AND THE BEER UPRISING

Did you know that until 1967 barmaids were banned in South Australia? Most other states had hosted anti-barmaid campaigns, and while they were not successful in New South Wales (in 1884 a bill was defeated by just one vote) or Western Australia, they were in South Australia and Victoria.

In Victoria 346 licences were issued in 1885 to barmaids as a means of ending the pernicious practice of allowing women to serve beer. The licensed girls were to be the last of their kind. The Vics eased the regulation as a temporary measure during World War Two but publicans forgot to sack them when the boys got back. Thank God.

Everyone has heard of the Eureka Stockade but in 1918 beer restrictions led to the most serious and prolonged civil disobedience campaign ever witnessed in Australia.

The Federal Government ran Darwin's hotels after World War One and imposed laws which restricted people taking beer away from pubs and then raised the price by threepence.

A boycott was declared and in December 1918, 1000 men stormed the administrator's office demanding the man be sent away on the first steamer. The administrator was manhandled, his assistant lost his trousers and an effigy was burnt. That administrator left town, as did another six months later, along with his secretary and the judge of the Supreme Court.

This was a serious issue and eventually the drinkers prevailed.

A SAD END

The story about the man drowning in a vat of beer at the brewery has made its way into folklore. However, there may just be some truth to it.

In the 1890s a brewer named Joseph Hartley was found floating in a tank of beer at the Castlemaine brewery in Victoria. He was dead, although it is not known if he had fought off any attempts to save him.

The customs officers and health authorities insisted the beer be run off down the street gutters and a broken-hearted group of spectators gathered to watch.

One paper at the time suggested that Hartley had become 'too much absorbed in his business'.

The Bulletin magazine published a poem at the time, bemoaning the loss of the beer and Hartley. In part, it read:

For poor old Joseph Hartley,
The poet sighs, or partly,
And likewise drops a tear.
But not for Joseph only,
In the graveyard lying lonely.

Doth the poet drop a tear,
So crystal, bright and clear
He is thinking, thinking, thinking,
Of that liquor brewed for drinking.

BOB HAWKE'S RECORD

Politicians are remembered in history for all sorts of contributions: wars, corruption, sex scandals, economic mismanagement, taxes, total bastardy, ignorance, sloth, greed . . . but one got his name in the textbooks for the right reason — beer drinking.

Our own Rhodes Scholar in Canberra, the right honourable former prime minister Bob Hawke actually made history even before he took the top job.

As a young man at Oxford, the knock-about soon-to-be union leader was called out at the dining hall of his college for not wearing a gown. As part of the college rules he was obliged to down two and a half pints of British ale in less than twenty-five seconds. According to Bob's memoirs, failure to do so meant he would have to pay for the first drink and then another.

Bob was a politician even in those days and didn't think he should have to fork out his own hard-earned money for a beer, so he took on that ale like his life depended upon it. Terrified of reaching into his pocket, the young Aussie student knocked back the lot in eleven seconds. The effort was recorded for history in the *Guinness Book of Records*.

Bob's record stood for some time, but we have heard about a young fellow called Leo Williams from the University of Queensland who put our Hawkie to shame. Representing the law faculty, the young man took on the whole campus in a drinking competition.

Leo almost broke the laws of physics by downing 2.6 litres in an incredible 7.9 seconds.

Apparently, a guy called Harold Fulton managed to drink thirty pints of beer in Sydney in the 1960s during an eight-hour session. He only had one leg too!

BREAKFAST OF CHAMPIONS

At any given time the sun is over the yardarm in some part of the world, but for brewers it's never too early to have a drink. These hearty souls not only make the beloved liquid, some include it in their breakfast.

Here's a little recipe for a brewer's breakfast. It's not quite hair of the dog, more of a lining for the kennel.

THE BREWER'S BREAKFAST
one bowl of toasted muesli
one cup of hot wort straight from the mash (unhopped)
half a cup of fruit
one cup of yoghurt

Pour into schooner glass, hold nose and drink in one swill.

The answers to life's problems aren't at the bottom of a beer bottle, they're on TV.

Homer Simpson

CRICKETERS

Remember the great days of the Australian male? Remember when real men wore moustaches without fear of any confusion in a public toilet? Remember the Aussie bloke and his beer-drinking exploits? Remember our cricket side when every single bloke was a fair-dinkum-knockabout-larrikin who was pretty good on the field but much better in the pub?

Not that long ago the Australian cricket team made most builders' labourers look like synchronised swimmers. Back then the great challenge for our first XI wasn't facing the fearsome Windies, or even deciding which open-necked paisley shirt went with which slacks; no, it was how much beer you could drink.

And if the Ashes were the ultimate in cricketing tradition, then the Australia–England jet-plane beer-drinking record ran a close second.

For many years it was held by the laidback Doug Walters, a man who could knock up a ton, drop a bit of money at the races, and smoke half a pack of fags between lunch and tea.

It's alleged Doug once stunned the whole side by announcing he was going to 'warm up'. Nobody hated practice more than this naturally talented New South Welshman. Having made the statement, Doug arose, threw two darts at a dartboard, and sat down.

Warmed up.

In 1977 Doug Walters sat down for forty-four cans of beer on a flight between Sydney and London, a mark most considered unbeatable. Asked about this recently, Dougie told *Inside Edge* magazine a little about the flight.

'Rod and I used to sit together and have a drink on the plane. Now we got some good service in those days and we set some records that I don't think will be broken for a long while — you can't get that sort of service on a plane these days.'

Doug reckons it took a concentrated effort to establish the record and he didn't dare sleep.

'No way, mate. You can't sleep and drink at the same time.'

Then Rod Marsh, the West Australian wicket-keeper who looked like the progeny of a wrestler and a walrus, decided that he was going to set his own record. At five foot eight and a half inches, Marsh was heavy-set and had classic beer-drinker's legs: each one looked like it could — and on some occasions did — hold a keg of beer.

Rod always claimed that he had matched Doug beer for beer on the recordbreaking 1977 flight where he had acted as pace-maker, but nobody believed him. His chance to prove himself came in 1983 when the team was due to fly to London for the World Series in England.

Rod's best mate Dennis Lillee knew that the wicket-keeper was keen to have a crack, but secretly believed it wasn't a good idea. Now the fast bowler is no wowser himself, but he figured that it would be better to have somebody behind the stumps who hadn't died of alcoholic poisoning before landing in the Land of the Pom.

So, Dennis decided to get his mate well tanked before take-off. They drank on the red eye special all the way from Western Australia, kept going at an official cocktail party in Melbourne and then really hit their straps when they landed in Sydney the night before their departure for England.

The plan worked a treat and everybody was crook as a dog the next morning, but just to make sure, the fast bowler lured Rod in for a couple of dog hairs before the flight. Three to be exact — and they weren't to be counted as part of the trip.

To make an attempt on any record takes a lot of preparation and planning and this record was no exception. The flight took twenty-four hours in three legs: Sydney to Singapore, Singapore to Bahrain, and Bahrain to London. That's fifteen cans a leg and two cans an hour if you're going to beat the record.

Despite his mate's best attempts at sabotage, Rod pressed the hostie button the moment the wheels left the ground in Sydney. The hostess was informed of the plans and said that she would help in any way possible.

Apparently he was drinking Fosters, and although it sounded like he was speaking English as a second language, he was right on target when the plane touched down in Singapore. Graeme Wood was keeping score and had the little fella down for fifteen cans.

It was illegal to drink during refuelling — something to do with volatile fumes mixing with the avgas — and the moment they touched down Rod passed out.

Lillee relaxed; his plan had worked and his mate couldn't keep up the pace.

But he had underestimated the guy, who was one of the greatest keepers of all time, for the moment the plane was in the air again Rod was alert and drinking and put away fifteen more on the next leg.

In his book *Over and Out*, Lillee claims that he fell asleep on this leg and was horrified to wake in Bahrain and see that his mate had put away thirty cans. Admittedly Marshy was now talking in an obscure Arabian dialect, but like a good keeper, he hadn't missed a chance and was well on the way to the record.

When the plane touched down the little fella went quiet, apparently having passed out.

Of course, the moment that old plane took off Rod was back at it again and by this time the whole economy section was following the mammoth innings taking place high in the skies above the northern hemisphere. This was Bradmanesque — not that the teetotalling Don would have approved.

Even the captain joined in and made an announcement about the record attempt to those who hadn't already caught on. In those days responsible service of alcohol meant you could serve anybody who could remember their name or knew somebody who once remembered their name. Back then the only time you were too drunk to drive was when you couldn't find your car; and our man had no intention of driving anywhere, so they just kept those beers coming.

Anyway, the tally kept rising and Lillee swears that as the plane tilted for its descent towards Heathrow, beer started to spill over his mate's bottom teeth.

As they approached the airport, can forty-four arrived and was eventually forced down before tragedy struck. The record breaking forty-fifth can came down the aisle and somehow Marsh indicated that he couldn't do it.

The runway was approaching almost as fast as the ignominious failure.

Back in those days a mate was a real mate and the rest of the team held his mouth open and somehow poured the beer down his throat. Although, if the truth be known it probably came to rest about a centimetre below his tonsils.

Rod Marsh had done it and there were delirious celebrations from everybody except the wicket-keeper, who was by now catatonic.

Woods and Lillee had to change him out of his drinking clothes and into the official ACB gear before hitting customs. They propped him between themselves and made for the gates, only to be caught by the lizards of the English press who had the temerity to suggest in the next day's paper that Lillee had been in on the game too.

If they only knew what a wowser he really was.

But there you have it — Rod Marsh, beer-drinking champion of the Australian cricket team with an unbeaten forty-five-can London–Heathrow record.

Many claim David Boon later matched or beat this, but Boon denies it and we can find no reason to doubt him. Cricketers don't lie. Do they?

Merv Hughes says that Boonie knocked off fifty-six cans on a flight to London. Walters argues that Boon is not in the running for the record because he counted the ones he drank in the terminal.

Boonie spoke about the record recently and said that it was 'a fairytale'. When asked how many he really had he said, 'Oh mate, you can make whatever mark you want. When you're having a beer, who counts?'

Why don't Channel Nine do a commemorative print of the lads' famous feats? There'd be plenty who'd be proud to hang that on the wall of the home bar. I can hear Tony Greig's sales pitch now: 'This wonderful commemorative print captures the moment the . . .' Oh well, maybe not.

AUSTRALIA TO LONDON UNOFFICIAL BEER-DRINKING RECORDS

1977	Doug Walters	44 cans
1983	Rodney Marsh	45 cans
1993	David Boon	56 cans (unconfirmed)

DEAD DRUNK

There's a story doing the rounds about a thirty-three-year-old Australian who won some sort of drinking contest, but at enormous cost.

This bloke, who worked in the computing industry but didn't have quite as many megabytes of hard drive as you'd expect, keeled over after drinking thirty-four glasses of beer, four bourbons and sixteen tequilas in one hour and forty minutes. His blood alcohol was apparently .353. That's more than seven times over the limit and way past a man's ability to keep alive, let alone drive.

Our computer geek was partaking in a drinking competition which gave contestants 100 minutes in which to consume as much alcohol as possible. Under the rules of the competition, you were awarded one point for a beer, three for a wine and eight for a spirit. Our man scored 202 — the equivalent of 202 beers in 100 minutes — and won the competition by 44 points.

Unfortunately, he died before he could collect the prize and the barman was fined $20,000 for his part in the stupidity.

The difference between a drunk and an alcoholic is that a drunk doesn't have to attend all those meetings.

Arthur Lewis

FISHY STORY

Believe it or not, anthropologists believe the human race has survived until now because it drank beer.

Back in the time when water was a carrier of the Black Plague and all sorts of disease, even the churches recommended that people drink ale (the only known beer in the early days). Apart from the fact that the church owned the breweries, they also knew that the water in it was boiled and sterilised.

Anthropologists reckon that people in the West developed a capacity for grog during these times, while the gene pools of Asia were saved by a taste for tea, which is apparently also made from boiled water.

The earliest recorded mentions of beer date back to 6000BC. There's even some thought that civilisation began when the old-timers began to harvest the first crops — in order to make bread and beer. The words have the same origin and beer was once made after the grains were baked into a bread-like form which was then able to be soaked in liquid.

While it would have been pretty rough to drink and people probably used straws to filter the crap out, at least it kept you alive and happy. Some time later people realised that bread filled in a few gaps as well.

These days the water's clean, except that fish fornicate in it, and now it appears that there could even be fish and pig gut in beer. Animal liberationists, People for the Ethical Treatment of Animals, launched a campaign warning that some beers contain pepsin, a protein from pigs' stomachs that makes beer frothy.

There is also a concern that brewers are using fish bladders to clean the impurities. And they're right; there's a product called Isinglass, made from fish bladders, which is used to remove the yeast from beer.

Now you know!

MEATY DROP

A lot of good beers and breweries have come and gone since white man first built a pub on these shores. Then again, a lot of forgettable crap has gone the same way.

One brewer wrote to the *Australian Beer Journal* in March 1895 with details of his remarkable new recipe for an ale which he claimed 'will be a valuable medium for supplying nourishment to persons who are in ill health and unable to take food in its solid form'.

Yeah, right.

The brewer's recipe involved adding fifteen pounds of calves' heads or feet, ten pounds of bullocks' heads and shins of beef, two bushels of malt, twelve pounds of hops and five grains of quinine to every brew.

One can only imagine that a vegetarian plot undermined this ingenious recipe and stopped it becoming as Australian for beer as, well, you know.

Beer is proof that God loves us and
wants us to be happy.

Benjamin Franklin

PUB WITH NO BEER

Everybody has heard the song, but did you know it is based on a real-life tragedy?

There have been some dark days in Australian history, but none so bleak as that terrible time that Ingham boy Dan Sheahan arrived at the Day Dawn Hotel after a hard day's work only to be greeted with the news that the pub had no beer as American servicemen had drunk it dry.

The Yanks' troop convoys had passed through town and shown scant regard for the quota system which was in place at the time because of the war. And they were supposed to be on our side!

With a tear in his eye, Dan accepted a glass of wine and retired forlornly to the parlour and began to write a poem.

The late Gordon Parsons, singer-songwriter and timber worker from the Kempsey area, changed the lyrics a little and set them to the tune of an 1862 American folk song by Stephen Collins Foster called 'Beautiful Dreamer'.

Slim Dusty recorded the song 'The Pub With No Beer' and the rest is history . . . well, almost.

You can find The Pub With No Beer at Taylor's Arms, near Kempsey, New South Wales, but Queenslanders reckon that Ingham's Lee Hotel, which is on the site of the old Day Dawn Hotel, is the real McCoy.

RUSSIA AILED BY BEER

You've got to love those Russians; they just seem to have a thirst for the hard stuff that leaves most of us looking like bloody great nancies.

In January 2001 the Russian Health Ministry launched a campaign for beer to be recognised as an alcoholic drink. For some strange reason the Russkis never considered the amber stuff to be alcoholic and so even children could buy and drink it.

The idea was that if it was readily available people would drink less vodka, but it seems the locals just drank vodka and beer.

The mayor of Moscow even authorised the building of a large brewery outside the city saying that beer was the perfect cure for recovering alcoholics.

Sounds like the sort of politician we need.

WAR STORIES

A BELLYFUL

During my first tour of duty in Vietnam (1967–68) we were under the old rule of one beer per man per day. In an effort to 'savour' the event, we would drink them a little faster than normal and then lie down on the sandbag bunkers and let the sun warm up the belly.

After a few minutes you would stand up very fast. The reaction was like that of smoking your first cigarette and getting very dizzy. Short-lived, but something to look forward to the next day!

Butch Brown

A CASE OF VD

A navy ship had been in an exotic port for a couple of weeks when the captain ordered all the crew together.

'Gentlemen, I am disturbed to have to say that we have discovered quite a few cases of VD on board the ship,' he said.

'That's good,' said one of the sailors.

'What could be good about that?' asked the captain.

'Well,' said the sailor, 'it's got to be better than the local beer.'

Brian Wallace

A FOSTERS OR AN ABBOTTS

I was serving with 6th Battery, 2/3rd Field Regiment and at our first position in Greece we were issued with two bottles of beer. The signals sergeant did the issuing but had some bottles left over as they couldn't be sent to observation posts etc.

When we were forced to withdraw, some infantry men stopped and gave covering fire while our guns were timbered up, then hopped onto our trucks. A couple got into a signals van. One of them said, 'How'd a beer go now?' and nearly fell out of the van when a sig produced two bottles and said, 'Which one do you want, a Fosters or an Abbotts?'

Neil Gillies

KOREAN HOPSICLES

During the Christmas of 1953 I was a young soldier/cook serving in Korea. The practice of the government was to issue soldiers with a beer ration on days such as Christmas Day, ANZAC Day etc.

Two bottles of Abbotts lager were issued per soldier for Christmas Day; they were to be consumed with lunch in an effort to improve morale.

The intense cold (minus fifteen degrees centigrade) caused the beer to become somewhat frozen and great difficulty was experienced in attempting to consume the much anticipated brew.

As it was so cold, many soldiers were gathered around my field stove and some bottles were placed on top of the range where the bottoms became heated a little. Soon the heat began to force the beer up through the neck of the bottles like a candle-shaped periscope.

The diggers then proceeded to chew lumps from the beer candles as they rose from the bottle like some kind of hopsicle. As the beer warmed too much, the bottle was placed in the snow to refreeze and the process was repeated.

What a Christmas! And those memories are recalled each ANZAC Day as the tastiest Christmas candles ever invented.

This now old cook still likes a cold drop on a hot day.

Dudley C Pye

BEER PYRAMID

I was in the RAAF in Vietnam (Caribou Transport Flight at Vung Tau) in the very early days of our involvement in the war (June 1965). Our access to any beer other than the local 333 was nil.

As secretary of our little 'club' at the villa I had heard that in Saigon the Americans had a warehouse full of beer (used to supply their Special Forces camps).

So, armed with a fistful of US dollars and a helper, and with the cooperation of the pilot of one of our Caribous, it was arranged that we (and the beer — about sixty cartons) would be picked up at the Ton-Son-Aut (Saigon airport) at about 4 p.m. one afternoon.

Everything went very well and we were in position on the tarmac at 2 p.m. with the beer.

We couldn't leave our prize, but to fill in the time my helper suggested we build a sort of pyramid out of all the cartons. It looked great.

At 3.30 p.m. a tropical rain storm hit us and dumped approx one and a half feet of water on us and the pyramid of cartons. There was hardly a carton which was not soaked. Our Caribou arrived on time and we loaded the beer a can at a time, as each carton fell apart as soon as you touched it.

The unloading at Vung Tau was the same — one can at a time out of the plane and one at a time into a truck and again a can at a time at the villa.

The beer by now was hot and undrinkable due to the way it had been thrown about. After we'd chilled the beer (for twenty-four hours) everyone enjoyed a better-quality brew.

I did the same trip to the Saigon warehouse every two weeks for the next six months, except I had a very heavy large tarpaulin and a helper who was content to sit on a square block of cartons for however long it took.

Fred Fortescue

Always do sober what you said you'd do drunk. That will teach you to keep your mouth shut.

Ernest Hemingway

UNOPENED BEER AND DUNNY DOORS

Back in the early 1970s when I was serving on HMAS *Melbourne*, our mess had a soft drink fridge. Cartons of soft drink were purchased ashore and the fridge was kept full of various types. Payment for each drink was via an honesty box and any profits went towards a mess party at some overseas port.

Before leaving Sydney for exercises off Hawaii I was elected to be drinks purchaser and I duly purchased large quantities of Tarax Black Label drinks (now there's a blast from the past).

At Pearl Harbor I went off to the local PX to restock our supplies and was confronted by a number of brand names that I hadn't heard of. I purchased cartons at random, later carrying them as bold as brass with a few of the blokes up the gangway and down into the mess.

At sea a couple of days later, we discovered that the lemonade in the flashy blue cartons was in fact PABST beer. Needless to say it was secreted away — smuggling booze on board was a big no no — to be enjoyed on the last night before hitting Sydney.

And what a night it was.

When at sea on *Melbourne*, each man was entitled to one 26oz (750ml) can a day, provided there was no night flying that night.

We were in a petty officers mess (senior sailors) and as such a couple of mess members would collect a can for every member. Any non-drinker's can would be stored away for the last night party before getting home.

The powers that be were aware of these lurks and when they were collected the cans were 'cracked' (back in the days of the ring pull). This was always done for junior sailors, but it was overlooked for senior sailors as a sort of unofficial privilege of rank.

This practice came to the attention of a very strict and straight 'Master at Arms' (the ship's head policeman) nicknamed The Hat (sailors from the 1970s will know who he was). The Hat ordered that senior sailors' cans were to be 'cracked' before issue. This almost caused a mutiny amongst us and there was much bitching and moaning.

I can remember one old salt saying that the only privilege senior sailors had on this ship was 'unopened cans of beer and longer shithouse doors!' (junior sailors had half length doors, senior sailors three-quarter length and officers full length).

The next morning some wag got hold of a texta and drew dotted lines on the doors of the senior sailors' toilets (heads) near our mess, with the words 'cut here'.

Andrew McCarthy

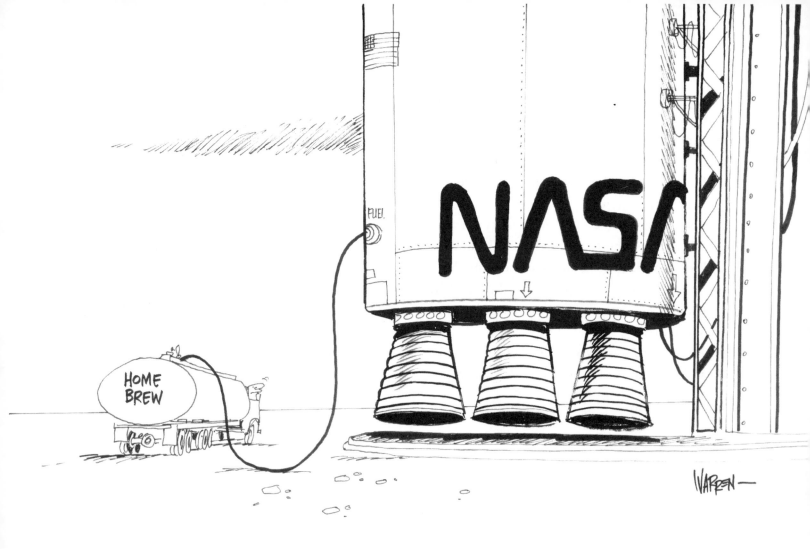

HOME-BREWERS

A BEERY CONFESSION

In the late 1970s I worked for a large company in Sydney. During our lunch breaks a lot of the men got together in the canteen (or sometimes down the local). The conversation varied from sport to eating and drinking.

At the time home-brewing was big in the suburbs, particularly among the married men. Being single, I had better things to do with my time and money.

Naturally each person reckoned his brew was the best and tasted like the real thing. They often brought samples for me to try. Not wishing to offend, I told them it was hard to tell the difference; home-brew is home-brew — and nothing has changed if you ask me.

Anyway, the boys decided they would have a home-brew barbecue at Browny's place. Everyone had to bring six 750ml bottles of their finest for judging by the experts.

Not wanting to be left out, I put down a brew from one of the many recipes given to me. I'll be honest: it was nearly undrinkable.

On the day of the big event, I bought three large bottles of KB and three bottles of Tooheys Flag Ale, removed the labels and replaced the tops with my plain crown seals.

For a start my two beers caught everyone's eye because there was no sediment; the old-style home-brews were loaded with it.

Then the taste really got to them.

I was going to own up at the end of the day but I got in so deep with all my secrecy and fibs that I had to go on with it.

For months after the event my brews were discussed reverently and my mates tried to make me give up my secrets, but to no avail.

I no longer have contact with those guys so you can let 'Feet's' secret out of the bag if you want — sorry Browny and the Eveready Gang.

I hope you will forgive me.

Anonymous

BAD OLD DAYS

Mine is a vintage tale dating back to over fifty years ago, the late 1940s, not long after World War Two, when beer was scarce indeed. These were the heady days of the 'six o'clock swill', when if you didn't tip the barmaid threepence a drink at the rare hours when the beer was 'on', you became invisible and didn't get another drink.

Bottled beer was a ration of two bottles per week, but only if you were a regular and qualified for a voucher.

My friend Bob and I decided to brew our own to save all the running around from pub to pub, only to find when you got there that the keg had just run out and there was no more. We were single young blokes and Bob's parents lived at the time in a short street that backed on to the Royal Manly Golf Course.

Bob and I resided in the garage at the back of Bob's parents' house, where we set up our own 'brewery': two four-gallon kerosene tins with the tops cut out held our special brew. On waking each morning, our first job was to inspect the magic potion and scoop off any mosquito wrigglers that had made their appearance overnight. When we considered it ready to bottle, we did so with the recommended amount of sugar and stored it in the cool under the main house for a couple of weeks.

Approaching the first bottle with some trepidation, we found it was drinkable, which was about the best that could be said of it.

Some well-meaning soul told us to double the sugar in the next batch, because this would give it 'a bit of a kick' and make it taste better. So we did just that.

We stored it under the house in the usual manner. However, one night Bob's mum came down to the garage, woke us and said, 'Whatever's going on with your beer I don't know, but there is a lot of noise. It woke me up. Please go and have a look.'

Sadly, most of our bottles had self-destructed and the area was an unholy mess. That was our last attempt at home-brewing.

Good old days, my eye! Now we can sample wonderful beers from all over the country, all over the world for that matter. I have been fortunate enough to have been able to sample many beers from many countries, without ever having left Sydney and its environs. In my opinion, some of our own beers must rate with the world's best: Squires, Dogbolter, Moonshine (Victorian) and Balmain Bock (which I hear is no longer brewed), to name only a few which come to mind. Our wonderful brewers in this country have produced lots more which I anticipate tasting before I fall off the perch.

Kevin J Crouch

CAT-A-TONIC

I've seen beer do strange things to men and women, but nothing like what it did to our family cats.

Patch and Ribs (mother and son) were feline residents and part of our family, commanding full attention as to food requirements and hours of leisure. In fact, leading a perfect cat's life.

I was in my learning mode for home-brewing a few years back and had obtained all the ingredients separately, mixing up a concoction from a recipe given to me by someone who knew someone who knew something about home-brewing. Or at least that was the story. This was in the days before home-brew shops and kits.

For this particular brew I decided to put half in 750ml bottles and half in 375ml stubbies. For some bizarre reason (I wonder if it had anything to do with beer) my teenage son begged to help me and after I recovered from the shock I put him in charge of adding the sugar prior to bottling and gave him precise instructions on how to do it.

Task completed, we put the bottles onto shelves in the external laundry for the secondary fermentation. Coincidentally, this was Patch and Ribs' boudoir.

Two weeks after bottling the brew I went into the laundry to let the cats out for the day. An unusual sight confronted me. Two cats, oblivious to their surroundings, were walking at virtually half their normal height, scraping the ground, their eyes glazed, racing in forward motion with only their toes moving (the same as cartoon cats on the TV), desperate to escape as quickly as possible from their house of horrors.

Evidently through the night the 375ml stubbies, due to their thin glass walls, had been unable to hold the inner pressure and had exploded, causing a chain reaction, smashing about six bottles. Glass shards and beer was everywhere.

Imagine what it had been like for Patch and Ribs, settled in for the night when all of a sudden all hell breaks loose. It was Pearl Harbor in the laundry and they had no way of escaping and no idea about what was happening.

They were in shock — literally out of their minds with fear.

What caused the bottles to erupt?

My son had done what he thought was right and put the same amount of sugar into each bottle, causing a vigorous secondary fermentation in the smaller bottles. Who said teenagers don't listen?

The poor cats were not keen to sleep in the laundry that night; in fact, they even discovered a hitherto unknown ability to run backwards in order to escape.

Soon after, Patch died after being run over by the family car, although it was thought this might have been suicide. Ribs died of kidney failure.

It seemed neither had the will to go on. Talk about having the horrors!

Ken Evans

EXPLODING BEER BOTTLES

Everybody has heard about the Japanese attacks on Darwin and the invasion of Sydney Harbour during World War Two by mini submarine, but a few of us were involved in a little-known battle in our suburban street.

During World War Two, our next-door neighbour made quantities of home-brew which he stored under the house. Late one night, loud explosions rocked the street. Our family and many neighbours raced into our backyard and down into our large air-raid shelter.

We huddled in the dark, fearing the 'invasion' had begun. During a long silence, some of the men ventured out and discovered smashed bottles and tops — the 'bombs' were cases of home-brew exploding amongst the foundations and against the floorboards.

Talk of 'having a beer' was greeted by sheepish grins and laughter for some time afterwards. (But, of course, a lot of beer had to be 'disposed of' — read that as 'consumed' — in a hurry 'in case it goes off again, mate!')

Elaine Johnston

HARD TO SWALLOW

I was having a drink with this home-brewer at the local pub when the publican called last drinks.

We'd put a few away but needed a roadie to clear the head. This was in the bad old days when bottle shops closed earlier than banks and it was looking pretty bleak.

Jim — well, that's what I'll call him in an attempt to keep his guilt anonymous — suggested I go back home and try one of his home-brews.

Now, other blokes had done this in the past and those that had survived the experience described a drink that while alcoholic was so bad not even the most hardened alcoholic could come near more than one. It had the odour of month-old witches' knickers and a flavour not unlike the slops that you find at the bottom of an abattoir's wheelie bin after a hot day.

I must've been a bit more pithed than I thought because somehow I found myself on the way back to Jim's house.

His horrible old wife greeted us at the door with a face that would scare Mike Tyson and an order that we take ourselves out to the back shed and not bother her or her equally ugly sister. Fat chance of that.

Anyway, Jim was also pleased to be banished to the shed and so we slunk through the house and made for the backyard.

Out in the shed he opened the fridge like a man opening a treasure chest. I swear the bottles were squirming and seething on the shelves and there appeared to be a foul green gas rising through the corroding tops.

Jim grabbed a bottle and then reached in the drawer for a bottle opener and a gun.

Yes, a gun.

Shit, I thought, he's gonna kill me.

'Don't be frightened,' said Jim. 'This is just to make sure we both have a nice drink.'

I was absolutely petrified as I didn't really know him that well and I was even more scared when he poured out a huge glass of this bubbling, burping, stenching, farting liquid and told me it was all mine.

'I, I, I, I might have lost me thirst, mate,' I said. 'I think I might've copped a poison pizza back at the pub.'

Jim went all strange and quiet. He looked at me, pulled the hammer back on the gun and pointed it at my temple.

'Drink the beer,' he said.

Trembling and gagging I raised the glass to my lips and apologised to God for being such a useless specimen, adding that I would never again get drunk, ignore the wife or ogle women if He let me out of this spot.

God is a bastard and I was forced to knock back the home-brew. Knowing not to sip, I threw it all down in one gulp.

I started to shake and sweat and everything spun for a while, but somehow I stayed on my feet and, despite feeling like a rat was decomposing in my stomach, I realised I was going to live.

Jim looked quite pleased about this and seemed to relax.

'Okay,' he said. 'Now it's your turn to hold the gun while I have a glass.'

Brian Noyes

HOMIES

Hidden in sheds and cellars around this beer-loving country is a strange breed of man, and the odd woman. Like mad scientists they hover over steaming vats, mix strange-smelling exotic potions, and pace the boards anxiously waiting for their creations to take life.

They are home-brewers and they are not like other people. They're obsessive, devoted, generally bloated and usually pretty bloody good people.

Up Bathurst way there is a thriving gang of homies who are so dedicated to beer that you'd think they had discovered a new religion. Come to think of it, the Church of Beer would have some appeal!

The treasurer of the Bathurst club, Big John, is a man who knows that a good brewer needs to be able to control his fermentation and lagering temperatures. In Bathurst the mercury is up and down more often than a unisex toilet seat and so something had to be done to keep Big John's brews in good shape.

Sparing no expense, he went out and bought a top of the range air conditioner and had it fitted to the small shed by the carport.

The only problem was, Big John's long-suffering missus had sweltered through the last thirty years in the house with only an electric fan for her comfort! Anyway, she soon got over it and was even allowed to go out and sit with the beer when the heat became too unbearable.

John, like the others, has converted a fridge into a mini pub. The boys just drill two holes in the door, fit taps and load the kegs inside. It's the perfect way to serve beer as you don't even have to open the fridge to get another coldie.

Another one of the homies, G, who hangs out with the Bathurst crew, bears the scars of his love for homemade beer. One night G was carrying a glass carboy filled with the precious fluid when it overbalanced and began to fall from his arms.

Now, a true disaster was on the cards.

No, G wasn't concerned about getting out of the way of the soon to be shattered glass that would surely explode like a bomb because of the gas inside; he was just keen to save what was apparently a top little ale and so he made a desperate lunge to save the batch.

Unfortunately, he failed and the breaking glass slashed his wrists and throat and he almost bled to death. Still, greater love hath no man . . .

You can imagine what sort of fishing trips the boys from the Bathurst home-brew club take. There's an absolute s−−−load of rods, reels, camping gear, food — and then there's the beer.

These blokes take two industrial-size freezers, a generator and on average about two kegs per man. Two blokes are on full-time bar duties roster and are expected to keep the beer in tip-top shape and make sure the lines and glasses are clean.

One of these years the boys reckon they might even catch a fish.

Peter Lalor

LOLLYWATER

A friend of mine, we'll call him B2 to protect his identity, recently went on holidays and left the keys to his shed with a good friend. We borrowed a bottle of B2's home-brew, drank the beer and replaced the beer with cold tea and put the bottle back in his shed fridge.

After B2 had returned from holidays he was telling me that he had taken a few home-brews around to a friend's place at the weekend.

He said his friend keeps his beer glasses in the freezer and when he poured the beer it partly froze and tasted like lollywater.

'I don't know what went wrong, but I could not drink it,' said B2.

I managed to keep a straight face during all this and B2 did not suspect any foul play.

A week later, a group of us were playing cards and I took out a bottle of cold tea from the fridge. When I poured it into B2's glass, he tasted it and said, 'Hey, the same thing must have happened to your beer.'

Ray Hardes

The problem with the world is that everyone is a few drinks behind.

Humphrey Bogart

NIGHTCAP

We own the Home-Brew Shop (and barbers) at Kincumber on the Central Coast and naturally get some funny tales from our customers.

Bill, one of our customers, had just started to make home-brew, but he found his first brew was too bitter, so instead of adding one kilogram of sugar he used two. This would achieve nothing, as the sugar converts to alcohol; he should have lowered the amount of hops. So the brew got stronger but not sweeter.

The beer was still too bitter for Bill so he added three kilos of sugar to his next brew, making it three times stronger.

When I asked Bill if the beer was any good he replied, 'Very good, only my wife insists that I put on my pyjamas and sit on the bed before I can have a schooner so she can just roll me over and cover me when I have finished my beer.'

Jim Ratcliffe

MOTHBALLS

Times were pretty tough during the war years for most families and ours was no exception, what with Mum, Dad and five kids to feed.

My dad always loved his beer, so he took to making his first home-brew. I believe it was a potent brew and we were forbidden to go into the back shed, as Dad would bravely enter each day to check how many bottles had exploded.

Six to eight weeks later the big tasting took place. Friends were invited in true Aussie tradition — everything was shared in those days.

There was great excitement as Dad poured everyone a drink and one for himself and Mum. As everybody took a sip a deathly silence descended and then someone mentioned mothballs, then another, then another.

Apparently in those days, at some stage you had to strain the brew. Mum had got out one of the clean blankets for the process, forgetting that she had stored the blankets in mothballs.

No one seemed to mind the mothballs taste as every last bottle was opened and drunk. I remember there were some massive headaches, but everyone lived to a ripe old age and kept coming to visit our home.

Forget the dot coms, the Internet, rockets to the moon. Remember good old Aussie tradition — a good beer, a barbecue and great friends. Our son is carrying on the tradition: he makes his own home-brew.

A great drop — without the mothballs.

Paulene Lowe

When I read about the evils of drinking,
I gave up reading.

Henny Youngman

OH DEAR, NO BEER

What a horrible feeling to be left without beer after a lousy day and, worse yet, being unable to buy any to rectify the situation.

Recently I had the pleasure of moving house and all our worldly possessions to a new suburb that we did not know very well. The weekend, which happened to be the Easter long weekend, had proved to be ideal.

I had enlisted two willing friends to help with the worst of the load with a reward of cold beer and a seafood lunch. After several round trips and plenty of effort, we had managed to get the job done without too much drama and all in time for the lunch I had promised.

All the seafood was ready, as were the appetites, but when I looked in the Esky for some beer to offer my friends I remembered that during all the packing up I had given away the remainder of my beer supply, thinking I would resupply rather than heave it during the move.

I was stunned and also embarrassed that I suddenly had nothing to offer my hired help. As it was Good Friday afternoon, I also realised I had absolutely no chance of buying any, no matter how desperate we were or how far I drove.

Enter the new next-door neighbour, who came by to introduce herself and had in her hand a plastic bag holding four longnecks of her husband's home-brew. It had high alcohol, a moderate head and was nice and cold.

I couldn't believe our luck. It was a just reward for the work we had done.

I have since replaced the beer to our generous neighbours and I have taken measures so I am never in that situation again, and I am always looking to extend my collection.

Hayden MacKellar

THE POSTIE

Home-brewing was popular in Sydney in the early 1950s. This was necessary to cope with the yearly Christmas beer shortages due to strike action by the unions seeking pay increases.

My father was reasonably good at the art, having been supplied with the proper ingredients, recipes and working instructions by a friend who happened to be one of the striking workers from Reschs brewery. Dad was popular with the neighbours, as he became the source of the only amber fluid to be had locally.

However, his fame was short-lived with the local postman, who said he would have 'contemplated murder' if he could have escaped uncaught.

Let me continue . . .

Postmen in those days did not zoom around on little Hondas; they had to make two mail deliveries daily on a push bike with a large leather mailbag over the front handle bars. It was customary for residents to give small Christmas gifts to the likes of the postman and garbage collectors for their diligent service throughout the year.

You guessed it — my father gave the postman two of his best brews. According to the postman's report the following day, both bottles exploded in his large leather mailbag after he had travelled less than 200 yards from our front gate. Ballpoint pens did not exist then and the ink-written addresses on the Christmas card envelopes had run.

The postman said he spent the rest of the day trying to dry out the envelopes and decipher the blurred addresses and NO he did not want the beer replaced. My dad never fails to recollect the story — 'Do you remember the postman blah, blah, blah' — as he samples my latest home-brewing effort.

John Gibbins

AUSSIES ABROAD

A BLESSED LIFE

I was on my first overseas flight, sitting in economy (a row of three seats). I was in the window seat, next to me was a Catholic priest and next to him was a Pakistani, who was a Muslim. We'd had several conversations when the subject of alcohol was raised and, most importantly, beer and religion.

The Pakistani asked the priest if he was permitted to drink beer.

The priest replied, 'It would be a bloody dull life if we didn't.'

Greg Rieper

BLIND DRUNK

On a trip to Europe back in 1983 we were staying in a caravan park near Hamburg. After getting settled we went to visit the nearby bottle shop and after much deliberation we decided to buy two cartons of 500ml stubbies of beer.

There were four of us and we were attracted by the novelty value of a half-litre stubby and the fact that it was the cheapest beer in the shop.

A party awaited!

We got back to the caravan park later that afternoon and started drinking and did not stop until the wee hours of the morning when almost all the beer was gone. The beer had contributed to a good night and we all slept like logs.

On waking the next day, all feeling a little seedy and sheepish, we'd started to clean up the empty bottles when the caretaker approached. We thought we might be in trouble for drinking all night, but the bloke just cleared his throat and said in broken English, 'Well done, you've probably just broken some sort of beer-drinking record. I've never seen anybody drink so much non-alcoholic beer.'

To say there were four red-faced travellers was an understatement.

Mark Dennis

COLLECTING GLASSES

My favourite beer yarn happened while my wife and I were touring Europe. We'd been travelling all over the continent enjoying foreign beers and, of course, collecting the usually quite decorative glass (as you do).

Whilst in Rome we went to a quaint little cafe and bar to enjoy a Peroni Nastro Azzurro or three. The glass looked quite collectable and it had my name written all over it. So I told my wife to whack this glass into her handbag, then we quickly left. Quite quickly, I might add.

Anyway, we'd gone about fifty metres down the road when the waiter came running after us, shouting something in Italian.

We looked at each other and thought, 'Should we run or face the consequences? I mean, what could they do? It's only a glass and we're dumb tourists who don't understand.' So we stood our ground.

The waiter came scurrying towards us talking very quickly in Italian. We were very worried.

Then from behind his back he pulled out our camera which we'd left behind in the rush.

We thanked him in the only Italian we knew — a tip.

We both heaved a big sigh of relief — but my wife gave me a serve over leaving the $400 camera for a $2 glass.

Kevin Bradley

Work is the curse of the drinking classes.

Oscar Wilde

COLOUR BLIND

Being fortunate enough to be twenty years old and travelling Europe, we decided we should not neglect our education. In no time at all we had become experts in all things beer: Czech beer, German beer, Belgian beer, Irish beer. We saw every day as a chance to learn and try something new.

So there we were in Paris, half a dozen Aussies, well behaved, some may have even described us as pleasant company. Well, someone thought so, as we found ourselves invited to — of all things — a wine tasting.

We went. We tasted some wines and generally tried to fit in; that is, until Rob decided to ask a question.

No harm in that, but when he wanted to say 'Is this a dry or a sweet wine?' Rob came out with 'Is this a red or a white wine?'

We left not long after that, found a pub we hadn't been thrown out of and enjoyed yet another wonderful evening helped along by good beer and great friends.

To this day none of us drink wine!

Gerard Meares

FOR GOD'S SAKE

Back in the middle of the 1970s I was in Belgium starting a new office for the company. Apart from Australia we also had offices in Houston, Texas and Tokyo, Japan at that stage.

One of the 'Good Old Boys' from the Houston office had cause to come over to Brussels for a period and one day we drove to Amsterdam to see a potential customer. We did whatever business we had to do and drove back to Brussels.

A kilometre or three from where we were living was a typical Belgian pub and we stopped there on the way home for a beer for the two of us.

The 'Good Old Boy' insisted on ordering, which he did in a loud voice: '*Dieu bieres s'il vous plait.*'

To which the barman replied in excellent English, 'You have just ordered God's beer.'

Quick as a flash the 'GOB' was back with, 'I know — for God's sake give us a beer.'

Jaak Jarv

GUINNESS FOR MOTHERS

The year 1982 was a very exciting time for my wife and me as it represented for us a series of firsts. Our first big holidays since we were married, the first time meeting our cousins and relatives, and the first time we had ever flown in an aeroplane. As one can imagine, we were in a state of great excitement by the time we boarded the plane at Mascot and after some six stopovers and thirty hours in the air we arrived at our destination — Holland.

This holiday on the other side of the globe was filled with excitement and wonderment and, given the short length of our vacation, we endeavoured to make every post a winner.

Having come so far, one of the absolute musts was to take a journey to the place of my mother's people, that being Ireland. Just getting to the Emerald Isle produced more stories than one might imagine, but the one I wish to recount occurred in County Clare.

Having arrived in Ireland we caught a train to our initial destination, where we established our home base in Mrs B Feeney's Bed and Breakfast, County Limerick. Following a minimum rest period we set about planning the best way to approach this fabled County Clare, given the limited resources at our disposal — namely, an empty pot of gold.

After considering our options it was agreed that we would travel in the most economical (and Irish) way possible: on shanks's pony. So, with purposeful strides we set off to discover the neighbouring county. According to the locals it was going to be one of those beautiful Irish occasions when the sun was to shine for the entire day, so consequently we were able to travel with a minimum amount of baggage, or in my case, garbage, as my wife would say. We walked for what seemed an eternity and by early afternoon our thoughts were beginning to remind us of the amount of slogging that would be required to complete the return journey.

On winding our way back to our lodging we passed a rather quaint little inn set well back from the road that had taken our fancy when we had passed it earlier in the day. Since I was yet to experience the sensation of a true glass of Irish Guinness stout I put forward the idea that given the circumstances I might break the drought in the inviting arms of the little tavern.

'But Max, we still have so far to go. Can't it wait until we get back to town?'

To this day I'm not sure how, but my body language must have suggested the urgency of my plea for I found myself leading my wife through the wooden doors of the pub without further protest.

Upon entering the premises we found the interior had both warmth and charm, with its heavily timbered walls and ceilings adding a feeling of grandeur associated with days gone by. A fine collection of Irish males was gathered around the bar, neatly attired in Donegal tweed coats and hats, who, we imagined, were completely oblivious to our presence as they continued on unabated in their various discussions.

We must have appeared like a pair of novices for as I was seating my wife at one of the tables a voice from behind caught my attention and I turned around to be greeted by a jovial Irish gentleman holding two pints of Guinness in his hands.

'Pat McNally's the name and I saw how you were both visitors [we must have stood out like sore thumbs] and how your lovely wife here is expecting [indeed, she was about six months expecting] so I'd like to say "Welcome to Ireland" and I want you to have a drink on me, particularly as your wife is expecting, 'cause y'know Guinness is good for mothers in child.'

With that he promptly left the drinks on the table and returned to the bar.

This gracious gesture on the part of our new-found Irish friend caused considerable alarm for my wife as she would never partake of anything stronger than the occasional glass of dinner wine and as a matter of course had chosen not to drink any alcohol during her months of confinement.

'But, Yvonne,' I protested, 'Pat would be offended if you refused his gesture of kindness. Look, you're just going to have to make the effort.'

After much deliberation and staring at the container my wife raised the glass to her lips and took a sip. The expression that came over her face suggested to me that she might be about to give birth right then and there.

'My God,' she choked. 'I'll just die if I have to drink this stuff.'

That terminated any further discussion on the subject.

Conscious of the need to satisfy custom and keep my marriage on the rails I made the bold suggestion that I would quickly drink my glass of Guinness and while no one was watching attempt the old 'switch-a-roo' and exchange glasses with my wife, thereby satisfying all parties.

Unfortunately for me someone was watching, for the next thing I knew there stood good old Pat with two more pints of Ireland's best.

'Pat, you shouldn't,' I protested. 'Really, we are very grateful for your kindness but we can't keep taking advantage of your hospitality like this.'

Pat would have none of this and after placing the drinks in front of us returned to be enveloped in the smoke and din that was being played out at the other end of the bar.

The scenario of the black medicine being good for mother and child routine was to go around two more times before the old 'switch-a-roo' was replaced with feelings of 'straight-to-the-loo'. With the double-barrelled prospect of an all-in domestic coupled with acute kidney failure, a joint decision (she decided, I complied) was taken and come hell or high water my wife was leaving.

It was then that the term 'legless' demonstrated its true meaning, for unlike my sober wife, whose path didn't deviate one step as she approached the door, my attempt at navigation resulted in my careering into every conceivable obstruction (including a now barking dog which had been sleeping under one of the tables).

Witnessing the untimely exit our friend Pat raced to the door to bid us farewell and, after the standard practice of exchanging information and addresses, took my hand and shook it vigorously and uttered these words that will live in my mind forever.

'Well, Max and Yvonne, it's been a pleasure to meet you and you never know, one day our paths may cross each other's again. But I've got to say one thing to you, Max, before you go — I don't know about you Australian men, but begorrah your women sure know how to hold their liquor!'

Max van den Berg

I am a drinker with writing problems.

Brendan Behan

ON PARADE

I went on a holiday to the USA in 1987, touring with a basketball buddy. We ended up in New Orleans in time for the big parade, only to find the 'Big Easy' wasn't as easy as they made out.

While we were watching the parade, we decided to have a quiet beer, only to find out to our amazement that it was illegal to have bottles or cans on the street.

We received this news from a friendly policeman who proceeded to take us into custody. Despite protesting our innocence and our ignorance of the law, it wasn't until we reached the police station that we were able to convince someone of the depth of our plight.

The desk sergeant realised that we were Australian tourists and took pity on us, letting us off with a warning and even offering to try to make amends. He was surprised when we declined his offer of buying us a drink.

Ray Mason

RASKOLS

I arrived in PNG in 1990 for a three-year contract. I enjoyed running and have always enjoyed a beer. Through work I met people from Hash House Harriers, a worldwide social running group. Beer consumption played a big part in the social activities. That didn't scare me, but the price of beer over there did.

I soon discovered that the way around this problem was to brew my own. I managed to put a kit together and put down my first brew.

A few weeks later I was having trouble sleeping so I decided to watch TV. It was 2.30 a.m. and I was starting to doze off.

Suddenly I was startled by a series of loud bangs followed by the sound of breaking glass. The house alarms were ringing and the dogs were barking.

I was quickly in a state of absolute panic and was lying on the floor trying to turn off the television and the lights.

I thought the local Raskol gangs were raiding the place. I figured they had let off some shots and would soon be coming over the eight-foot barbed wire fences.

Then I had another thought: The Beer.

I went to the back window, looked out cautiously and saw the majority of my first brewing effort running across the patio with glass strewn amongst it. My money-saving exercise had exploded in the most spectacular way.

The next Monday night that the Harriers met I was given a mug of beer to skol for wasting beer. After a few tips my following efforts were more successful and less stressful.

Garry Williamson

RUSSIAN LIGHTS

During my tour of Europe in 1990, I promised myself to try a local beer at every overnight stop — not an arduous task at all.

I settled down to a meal at a restaurant in Moscow and, as was my custom, asked the waiter for a local beer. He offered me typical black market goods — caviar, watches, military items — but seemed reluctant to bring me beer.

I persisted. I had been looking forward to a beer; it had been a full day touring and I was parched. 'Light beer,' I said, with my best Russian accent.

'Will you buy watch?' asked my entrepreneurial waiter — and I agreed.

That did the trick.

He brought to the table a 500ml bottle of Baltika No 9, which I thought was by far the finest light beer I'd tried. So good that I ordered three more. More than satisfied with my waiter's recommendation and in such a jolly mood, I purchased about $270 of the black market goods from him.

He too was obviously happy and shouted me one for the road.

Later I told our State tour guide that the waiter had put me on to this great light beer, but that it had a kick to it. I probably sounded a little Russian at that stage.

Boris the State tour guide (I kid you not) looked at the bottle, gave me a wry smile and told me that it was light in colour only — it had an alcohol content of eight per cent and then some!

I look back on that night with fond (if a little hazy) memories and to this day I have my Russian mementos (worth about ten dollars) as a reminder.

Paul Egan

THE TASTE TEST

During the early 1960s, I was living and working in London as well as playing Rugby Union for the famous London Irish Rugby Club. One evening, a representative from a major brewing company knocked on my door, inquiring about my level of beer consumption as well as choice of brand.

On learning my preferences towards beer, I was asked if I would be interested in taking part in a beer sampling study.

WOULD I WHAT?!?

I was informed that each week a representative from the brewing establishment would deliver twelve large bottles of different beer for myself and selected others to sample. The bottles came unmarked except that each had been inscribed with a letter ranging from A to L.

The task was simple. Drink the stuff and on the accompanying sheet mark the beers for levels of taste, clarity, colour and aroma, as well as the all-important alcoholic content.

Every Saturday the 'free liquid amber' was duly delivered to my abode and subsequently stored for later consumption. Of course, rugby was the usual agenda of the day (as was partaking in a beverage or two), and the after-match functions were always quite boisterous. As anybody from the era and area (Sunbury on Thames) would know, some of the times had in Fitzy's bar (The Nissan Hut) were quite an event.

The Rugby Club had built a new stand and bar; however, the concrete monstrosity lacked the atmosphere and heart of a good old London bar. The cold and impersonal stand and bar lay dormant as the parties raged on at Fitzy's till the wee hours.

Few of the boys owned cars (let alone were able to drive them) so we all had to bum a lift back to North London. The chosen few were invited back to my place for a glass or two of the free stuff, and after all the singing (which invariably included a few Welsh hymns) and dancing (especially after a match against the London Welsh) a drink or two were needed to quench the thirst.

In the words of the great Mr Bazza McKenzie we were all 'as dry as a pommie's towel'. And thus the sampling began. As you can imagine, six large Irish lads sampling and studying the finer points of this peculiar drop was a sight to behold (especially at two o'clock in the morning).

Needless to say, I had to spend the rest of the week filling out the form that had accompanied the brew. Hours and hours were spent calculating the high and low points of the flavour, fizz and nose of the last week's batch.

This frightful experience continued for twelve straight weeks. Handing back the empties, picking up the new and swapping over the information sheets was thirsty work, so as every Saturday rolled by, so did the chosen ones, to participate in tasting the new week's batch.

As word spread of our existence, the offers for lifts back up to NW2 (North London) became as common as the brew we had to pay for. However, as I was true to my friends, it was still the usual bunch who had the arduous job of polishing off twelve of the best each Saturday night (or perhaps Sunday morning).

It became obvious that our hard work had not gone unnoticed as the unnamed company came to the party, offering me another twelve weeks of their lager, which today has become one of the most popular lagers on the market.

Unfortunately — or fortunately — the rugby season had by this time passed so I was forced to drink the gold on my own. However, each time I decide that I might have a drop of the great stuff, it brings back some of the greatest memories of my time back in the Old Dart.

Maurice Kealy

I drink to make other people interesting.

George Jean Nathan

JOKES

Did you hear the one about the manager of a brewery whose sales were not as good as they could be? If the truth be known, nobody liked the beer.

Anyway, this executive decided that marketing was the way to sell more and he hired Brett Whiteley to paint a new picture that would encapsulate everything that was modern and cutting-edge about the beer.

Dear old Brett scratched a little and then came up with his painting of a couple going hammer and tongs on Bondi Beach.

Brett said nobody could see the picture until the company's big PR launch.

The manager got everybody together for the big event and the painting was unveiled.

'What the hell does that have to do with my beer?' asked the executive on seeing the work.

'Well,' said Brett with a laugh. 'It's f–––ing close to water.'

*   *   *

You heard about the brewery worker who fell into the vat of beer and drowned?

At the inquest the coroner thanked the man's colleagues for doing their best to save him and told the family it was a terrible tragedy but at least their relative died a quick death.

'Be buggered,' yelled one of his mates. 'It was a very slow death. He got out to piss three times.'

*   *   *

You heard about the blokes out fishing in a dinghy off the coast of Tasmania? One of them got his line snagged on something heavy and after a battle he pulled up a treasure chest. In the chest was an Arabian lamp, the sort that has genies in it.

So, the guy gives it a rub and, you guessed it, out pops a genie.

The genie perches on the bow and cuts to the chase.

'You've got one wish, get to it quick because I don't like it out here and I especially don't like boats.'

The fishermen are somewhat taken aback by the genie's demeanour and are disappointed that it is a bloke; nonetheless, one of the blokes has a bright idea and announces that he wishes the sea was made of beer.

Before you know it the genie is gone, the sea is a frothing mass of amber liquid and his mate is furious.

'You idiot,' he yells. 'Now we're going to have to pee in the boat!'

* * *

This bear walks into a pub and asks the mean-faced barmaid — a real bar bitch — for a beer.

'Sorry, mate,' she says. 'Don't serve people without shoes on. Bugger off.'

So the bear gets up and walks out but is back in a few minutes with a pair of shoes on. He sits at the table and asks the mean-faced barmaid for a beer.

'Look, you've got shoes on and that's good, but you ain't wearing a shirt so bugger off, there's no beer for you,' she says.

So the bear goes out and comes back in a tuxedo, with a top hat and nice shoes, and thinks to himself that this time the mean-faced barmaid can't possibly refuse him service.

'Can I have a beer now?' he says.

'No,' says the barmaid. 'To tell you the truth I can't stand bears.'

So the bear stands up, rips her head off and eats her.

Wiping the blood off his chin he walks up to the manager and says, 'Get me a bloody beer right now!'

'Sorry, mate,' says the manager. 'Can't serve people who take drugs.'

'Never taken a drug in my life,' says the frustrated and confused bear.

'Oh yeah?' says the manager. 'What about that barbituate?'

*   *   *

These three blokes have been out working on a building site all day when they decide to go for a beer. Unfortunately the local has been yuppified and the bouncer tells them they can't come in because they aren't wearing ties.

One of them pulls off his sock, ties it around his neck and fronts the bouncer again who lets him in.

The other grabs the belt from his trousers, ties it around his neck and he's let in.

The last bloke hasn't got socks or a belt so he runs back to the car and grabs the jumper leads and ties them around his neck.

The bouncer looks at him and says, 'You can come in, but don't go starting anything!'

*   *   *

This bloke walks into a bar and says to the barmaid, 'I'll have a schooner of lager, thanks.' He pays his money, knocks back the whole lot in one hit, burps and bellows 'Piss' before walking out.

Two days later he orders the same thing, goes through the same ritual and yells 'Piss' again as he leaves.

The next day the manager is waiting for him and before the bloke can order, the manager says, 'Piss off.'

'No problem,' says the man. 'I'll have a schooner of your ale then.'

*   *   *

Two little boys decide that they want to be like Dad. They both decide they will ask Mum for a beer and learn to swear. One gets the idea to say bloody while the other says shit.

So, when Mum comes into the room and asks them what they want the first says, 'I'll have a bloody beer,' and is duly beaten and sent to bed.

The second boy is then asked what he wants.

'Shit, I don't know, anything but a beer,' he says.

*   *   *

A bear walks into a bar.

    Barman: 'What can I get you?'

    Bear: 'I'll have a schooner of . . . beer.'

    Barman: 'Why the big pause?'

    Bear: 'Dunno. I was just born with them.'

* * *

A recent study has found that hormones in beer can turn a man into a woman.

    In a controlled situation a group of men were forced to drink fifteen schooners a day. Each put on weight, talked too much, stopped making sense, argued over nothing, became emotional, weren't interested in sex and had accidents in shopping centre car parks.

* * *

Did you hear about the alcoholic who got caught stealing twenty-two beers from a bottle shop?

    When dragged before the magistrate he said he should be let off because there wasn't enough evidence.

    'What do you mean?' asked the magistrate.

    'Well,' he said, 'if I'd taken twenty-four they'd have a case, but I'm not that stupid.'

* * *

I know I'm drinking myself to a slow death,
but then I'm in no hurry.

Robert Benchley

A particularly drunk bloke was walking home from the pub one night when he found himself near the local church. He entered and sat down in the confessional.

The priest waited for him to start confessing but the man just groaned, so the priest coughed to get his attention. This didn't work, so he banged on the grille.

'No use banging on the door, mate, there's no paper in here either,' said the drunk.

*   *   *

A couple of blokes were lost up in the snowfields and sure they were about to die. All of a sudden a kelpie came bounding over the pass with a small keg of beer around his neck, in much the same fashion as the famous St Bernards of the European Alps.

'Look at that,' said one of the blokes. 'Man's best friend has come to our rescue.'

'Yeah,' said the other. 'I think the dog wants to help too.'

*   *   *

A baby seal walks into a bar and orders a schooner of New.

The barman says that he doesn't get too many beer-drinking seals in his pub.

'Well, we're not about to order a bloody Canadian Club on the rocks, are we?' says the seal.

*   *   *

Which reminds me of the baby seal that walked into a club.

* * *

Then there was this dingo that walks into an outback pub and orders a beer.

The barmaid thinks she'll get the bludger back for the crimes of his relatives and demands $50 for the drink.

The dingo pays and then she says, 'You know, we don't get many dingoes around here.'

'At $50 a beer I'm not that surprised,' he says.

* * *

Q. Why do elephants drink?
A. To forget.

* * *

Q. Why do Queenslanders call their beer XXXX?
A. They can't spell beer.

* * *

Q. Why do Queenslanders call their beer XXXX?

A. They can't count to five.

* * *

There was this bloke who came from outback Queensland and he hits the big smoke, parking his ute outside a pub where he knows his mate's sister works.

He walks in and orders a beer and starts up a conversation with the girl.

They get talking and he pumps her for some information on what to do in the city.

She tells him about a couple of good restaurants and clubs and the like, but he seems nervous about going out by himself.

He then asks her to come out with him, but she's a city chick and he's a real bushie and she doesn't want to be seen out with him so she says no.

The bloke has obviously misread the girl.

Then he says, 'Listen, how about coming out with me tonight? I'll shout you dinner and the like and because it's been such a good year on the farm I'll give you $200 for your time.'

She doesn't want to, but thinks she could do with the money and so they go out and have a pretty good time, but she makes it clear that he'd better not get any fancy ideas.

The bloke then says that he's desperate for some, having spent so long on the farm that even the sheep have begun to look cute. He offers to chip in $300 for her time.

The girl has had a few and could do with the money so she figures why not, so they go back to her place and do it.

Afterwards she asks where exactly he's from and is amazed to find he's from the same farm as her brother.

'Wait until I tell him I met you,' she says.

'Yeah,' says the bloke. 'And make sure you tell him I gave you that $500 he owed ya.'

*   *   *

A young Kiwi bloke decides he's going to settle in Oz. Eager to fit in, he decides to forget about sheep and go along with the local customs.

The first night here he goes to a pub and meets a couple of regulars who get him pretty pissed. They then decide to have some fun.

'Mate, I'll give you $1000 if you let me smash a dozen full beer bottles over your head,' says one of them.

'I don't think so,' says the Kiwi, getting a bit nervous.

'C'mon, mate,' the rest of them say. 'We've all had a shot at this. It's part of Australian culture.'

'Well,' says the Kiwi. 'If it's a local custom I'll give it a shot. I've got a hard head and I could do with the money.'

So the local gets the dozen bottles and begins to smash them over the Kiwi's head.

It hurts like hell and there's blood dripping down the bloke's face but he hangs in there for the first eleven.

Then the Australian stops, opens the last bottle and walks away while swigging it back.

The Kiwi asks him what's going on.

'Well, I'm not a complete fool,' says the Australian. 'If I smashed this one it'd cost me $1000.'

*   *   *

This bloke walks into a bar and orders two beers. He sits down at an empty table, drinks one and pours the other on his hand.

He does this a couple of times before the barman asks what he's up to.

The guy blushes and then says, 'I'm just getting me date drunk before we go home.'

*   *   *

This flea walks into an empty bar, jumps up onto the stool and yells to the barman, 'Hey, mate, get us a beer would ya?'

The barman thinks he hears something but can't see anyone so he walks away.

The flea gets cranky and jumps up onto the bar and yells, 'Mate, get me a bloody beer. I'm dying of thirst!'

The barman looks down and sees the cranky flea, shakes his head and then gets the little bugger a beer.

The flea throws the beer up in the air, does a somersault and lands on his feet just as the beer pours out right into his mouth. He skols the lot and doesn't spill a drop.

'Another one, thanks, mate,' says the flea after letting out a rather large belch.

So the barman gets him another and the flea does exactly the same thing.

He does this time and again until he's run out of money and then the little bugger jumps off the bar and says goodbye.

The barman is still wondering if he hasn't dreamt the whole thing when the flea weaves his way back in.

'I thought you were going home,' says the barman.

'I would be, but some bastard stole me bloody dog,' says the flea.

* * *

This bloke's been at the pub all night and is totally tanked when the barman tells him to go home and sleep it off. After a bit of an argument and a little sulking the guy says, 'Well, bugger you then, I'll take my custom somewhere else!'

He gets off the stool and falls flat on his face. People rush to help him up but he tells them to 'bugger off' and tries to do it himself.

'God, I'm more pissed than I thought,' he thinks and giving up on the idea of standing he drags himself across the floor and to the door where he falls down the few steps to the footpath.

'I'll just lie here and get some fresh air,' he thinks, but even that doesn't work because every time he drags himself upright he falls down again.

Fortunately he only lives a few houses up the street so he just drags himself along until he gets to his front door.

Reaching up for the door knob he drags himself up so he can get the key in the lock and again falls down on his face.

Giving up on walking he drags himself down the hall, up onto the bed and next to his wife who mutters in her sleep about smelling like a brewery, being out all night, the dinner going cold and all that trivial stuff.

Before she can get a head of steam up the guy is asleep and so is she.

The next morning the missus wakes him early and starts again.

'You must've really tied one on last night,' she says.

'What makes you say that?' says the bloke whose head is hosting a private show by AC/DC.

'Well, the pub rang this morning and said you'd left your wheelchair behind again,' she says.

*   *   *

A drunk is making a bit of trouble in a pub so the barman decides to toss him out and bar him until he is sober.

The drunk weaves his way out the door and wanders around the corner where he finds another door so he goes in and orders a beer.

'I told you to go home,' said the barman.

The drunk is quite taken aback.

'How many frigging pubs do you own?' he spits on his way out.

* * *

A group of blokes are drinking in a pub when an old drunk comes up to one of them, stabs his finger in the guy's chest and says, 'Your mum is the best root north of the Mildura.'

Everyone thinks there's going to be a fight, but the bloke just ignores the drunk and turns to order another drink.

The old soak staggers off, only to return a little while later and confront the bloke again.

'I gave your mum one this morning and boy was she hot!'

The bloke gets angry but turns away without replying and the drunk weaves off across the bar again.

Sure enough, he's back again a few minutes later.

'Your mum gives the best . . .' Before he can finish the bloke explodes. 'For God's sake go home, Dad, you're drunk!'

* * *

Two mates were out on the turps having a pretty good night. They'd known each other since school days and even though one was university educated and the other was barely literate they got on pretty well.

The smart guy says he'd like to go out and maybe have a bit of slap and tickle.

'Good,' says the slower one. 'I know this bloody great club where you go in, have a couple of beers on the house, then go upstairs with whoever's arrived, have a root, go back down, have a couple more beers until somebody else arrives, then you go upstairs and have another root and so on until you've had your fill. Then when ya leave they pay ya.'

'I find that a little hard to believe,' says the smart one.

'Oh, it's true all right,' says his mate.

'Well, have you been there?' asks the other.

'Nah, but me sister has,' says the dumb one.

*   *   *

A family from the mountains of New Zealand decided after their twelfth child that they had enough children and maybe it was time to stop. Not knowing what to do, they went to the doctor and were told that the bloke could have a vasectomy.

After being told exactly what that was, the father of twelve decided he wasn't too keen on the idea. He asked the doctor if there was another option.

The doctor said they could stop having sex, but the wife was concerned that this might lead to problems.

Condoms were out because neither knew how to use them.

So the doctor suggested a method that had worked for Tasmanian hill families for many generations.

He told the man to go home, put a cracker in an empty can of beer, hold it in his left hand and count to ten.

The man said he couldn't see how such a thing would stop him having children but figured the doctor knew what he was talking about.

He went home that night and went out the backyard where he lit a cracker, put it in the can in his right hand and began to count.

2 3 4 5 . . .

Momentarily confused, he paused, then put the can between his legs and continued to count on the other hand.

7 8 9 10 . . .

Vasect Oh Me Oh My . . . that smarts!

*   *   *

A couple of very drunk old boys are sitting at a bar in one of the bohemian parts of the big city — one of those places where the men wear earrings and shave their heads and the women wear boots, shave nothing and roll their own.

Anyway, there's one of these urban girls sitting next to the old guys and she's wearing the standard uniform: singlet top, hairy armpits, torn jeans and boots.

The two men get friendly with the girl and figure she's all right and tell her just to signal the barman any time she wants a beer and it's on them.

So the girl raises her arm and the barman runs over and gets her a beer and this goes on for half the night: she raises her arm, gets a beer and the old guys pay.

The old guys are blotto by the time it comes for a last drink.

'Get the ballet dancer something from the top shelf,' says one.

'Ballet dancer?' says the girl quizzically.

'Well, anyone who can get their leg up high enough to order a beer musht be shome short of dancer,' says the drunk old man.

*　*　*

Have you heard the one about the three pieces of string who decide they want to experience the good life inside a pub?

The first two slick themselves down, straighten themselves up and walk up to the bar and ask for a beer.

'Sorry,' says the barman. 'We don't serve string around here.'

The third has hung back, and hearing that he figures he might try a different approach. He twists himself round into a knot and frays his ends before walking to the bar.

The barman is not impressed.

'Hey, I told your friends we don't serve string here; you are a piece of string, aren't you?' he says.

'Nah, I'm a frayed knot,' comes the reply.

* * *

There's a smart alec bloke at a pub who reckons he can tell any beer in a blind test.

So they put a blindfold on him and start bringing out different beers.

Boags, VB, James Squire . . . he picks them all until one wag comes out of the toilet with a glass of urine and puts it before him.

'That's p-p-p-piss,' splutters the smart alec.

'I know,' says the wag. 'But whose piss is it?'

* * *

Three businessmen meet in Sydney to discuss projections for the international company for the next financial year. One is from America, one from England and one is an Aussie.

After crunching numbers, planning mass sackings and boosting their executive entitlements the trio head for the nearest bar to wash out their mouths.

'I'll get you three local beers, eh?' says the Australian.

'Naw,' says the Yank. 'I'll have a Bud.'

'I'd prefer a pint of bitter,' says the Pom.

The Aussie turns around and asks for a pint of bitter, a Bud and a lemonade.

The others ask him why he hasn't ordered a beer.

'Well, if you're not drinking beer neither am I,' says the Aussie.

*   *   *

A drunk walks into a bar and takes the last bar stool right next to a rather proper old gal who's drinking a glass of wine.

The drunk orders a beer but soon the lady notices a terrible smell.

She turns to him and says, 'Excuse me, but I think you've pooped in your pants.'

'I shertainly have,' says the drunk.

'Well, why don't you run off and clean yourself up then?' says the lady.

'Yeah, yeah, I will, it's just that I haven't finished yet.'

*   *   *

A drunk walks into a pub and says to the bartender that he wants a beer but he's got no money.

The bloke tells him to bugger off.

'Hang on,' says the drunk. 'What if I show you a trick?'

'Well, it'd better be good,' says the bartender.

'Oh, it's good, in fact it's so good I think you should give me two beers.'

'We'll see,' says the bartender.

So the drunk carefully reaches into his pocket and draws out a green frog and places it on the bar. He then reaches into his other pocket and pulls out a miniature piano which he places in front of the frog.

The bartender is amazed, but even more so when the little critter starts to bang out the hottest jazz tunes he's ever heard.

Sure enough, the bartender shouts the drunk two beers.

When he's finished these, the drunk asks, 'If I can top that will you give me free beer for the rest of the night?'

'If you can top that you can have free beer for the rest of the week,' says the bartender, thinking that the pub will be packed with people coming to see the amazing jazz-playing frog.

The drunk smiles to himself and reaches into his pocket and pulls out a lady rat in a slinky dress. The rat leaps from his hand, leans against the piano and sings along.

The bartender is blown away and keeps his word. While the drunk drinks, the rat and frog entertain customers and the pub is packed every night.

On the last night of their deal a theatrical agent walks in and cannot believe what he sees.

He immediately offers the drunk $1000 for the frog and the rat.

'Nah, forget it,' says the drunk.

The agent then says he'll give $1000 for the rat alone.

'You're on,' says the drunk.

The agent takes the rat and leaves, but the bartender is furious.

'You just broke up a million dollar duet for a lousy $1000!' he yells.

'Don't worry about it,' says the drunk. 'The frog's a ventriloquist.'

* * *

This old geezer's lying on his deathbed, family gathered around and everyone is feeling a bit emotional.

Even his nagging wife is in a good mood.

'You've been a good husband,' she says. 'We've had a good life together. Is there anything I can get you, love? Any last request?'

'I don't want to be any trouble,' he says.

'Oh, sweetheart,' she replies. 'Everybody deserves a last wish. You just ask and I'll do my best.'

'Well, I would love one of those beers you put in the back fridge yesterday,' he says.

'Oh my God,' she says. 'Just like you — selfish and thoughtless. Those are for the wake!'

*   *   *

This drunk walks into a bar and says to the bartender, 'Give me a beer before the shit hits the fan.'

The bartender gives him a drink and walks off.

The drunk calls him over again and says, 'Give me another beer before the shit hits the fan.'

The bartender obliges and this goes on for a while before the bartender says, 'I hope you've got enough money to pay for these.'

'Oops, the shit's hit the fan,' says the drunk.

*   *   *

A Queensland cow cockie parks his ute outside a Sydney pub, grabs his swag and shotgun out of the back, goes inside, puts the gear down and has a big afternoon on the beer.

Towards evening he picks up his swag and shotgun and leaves, only to return a few seconds later red with anger.

He lets off a shot into the ceiling and yells, 'Somebody has stole me frigging ute and if it's not back by the time I finish me next beer I'm gonna have to do what I did in Melbourne!'

The locals pick the bits of ceiling from their receding hair and look at each other nervously.

The bartender gets the cow cockie a beer and starts to sweat when he notices the car park still empty.

'Will you tell me what happened in Melbourne?' asks the bartender.

'Yeah, I will,' the cockie says. 'I had to walk all the way home.'

They who drink beer will think beer.

Washington Irving

* * *

A wombat emerges from a building site and walks across the road into a pub and asks for a beer.

The bartender is taken aback to find a talking wombat.

They get chatting and the bartender asks where the wombat works.

'Over the road on the building site,' comes the reply.

'Well, you know with your skills you could get a job in the circus,' says the bartender.

'A circus?' asks the wombat.

'Yes, a circus,' says the bartender.

'One of those joints with tents, animals and sawdust?' asks the wombat.

'That's the one,' says the bartender.

'What would a frigging plasterer do at a circus?' asks the wombat.

* * *

A greyhound has just ordered a beer from the bar and is walking back to his seat when he overhears a group of racehorses talking.

'You know, I was at Flemington yesterday and the strangest thing happened,' says one. 'I was ambling along at the back of the pack, getting those bastard owners back for chopping off my you-know-whats, when all of a sudden I felt this red hot sensation up my dot like somebody had shoved a burning poker up it. Next thing I know I'm four lengths in front and I've set the bloody race record.'

'Same thing happened to me,' says another horse. 'I was at Randwick right at the back of the field when all of a sudden I got this incredible burning penetration up me bum and before you know it I'd won the race.'

The third says that the same thing had happened to a couple of his mates.

The greyhound then chips in and says, 'Sorry to intrude, guys, but exactly the same thing happened to me when I was racing a fortnight ago. I was coming last as usual, thinking they'd have to retire me after this effort, when all of a sudden I got that red hot poker feeling up me out chute and whammo I've won the bloody race.'

The horses all went silent, so the greyhound continued on to his table.

'Can you believe that?' said the horses when he'd gone. 'A talking greyhound!'

* * *

Three English backpackers were in a bar and spotted an Irishman among the locals.

One lad said he was going to get this guy worked up. He walked over to the Irishman and said to him, 'Hey, mate, your St Patrick was a bastard and a wanker.'

The Irishman put down his drink and the Pom backed off a bit, but then the bloke just turned away and said, 'Oh really, didn't know that. There ya go.'

The Englishman walked back to his mates quite crestfallen. 'I told him St Patrick was a right bastard and he didn't seem to care!'

'I'll show you how it's done,' the second Pom said and walked over and tapped the Irishman on the shoulder. 'I hear your St Patrick was a gay homosexual.'

The Irishman again put his drink down, thought for a second and replied, 'Oh, I didn't know that, there you go.'

The Pom walked back to his mates and said he couldn't get a rise out of him.

The third Pom decided he had the right stuff and told his mates to watch his form.

'I hear your St Patrick was an Englishman!' he said to the Irishman who replied almost immediately, 'Yeah, that's what your friends were trying to tell me.'

*   *   *

Which reminds me of the old joke about the Aussie, the Pom and the Scot. All three were drinking a beer outside in a beer garden when three flies flew down and landed in the beer.

The Pom said, 'I'm not drinking this, it's got germs in it.'

The Aussie just picked the fly out and kept drinking, while the Scot pulled his fly out by the wings and said, 'Spit it back, you wee thievin' laddie.'

An Irish bloke walks into a bar one Friday and asks for three beers. The bartender serves him and then watches as the bloke takes a sip from one glass, then another and then another, until he has finished all three.

The Irishman then goes back and orders three more.

The curious bartender asks him why he doesn't drink one at a time like everybody else.

The Irishman tells him that he's got a brother in Australia and one in America and they made a pact that on this day every year they would go to a pub in their respective parts of the world and drink a round or two to remember when they were together. It seems that they had been very close and had a drink every Friday since they were eighteen.

So, the Irishman comes back every Friday and does the same thing and everybody in the pub becomes acquainted with the strange ritual.

Then one Friday the bloke comes in and only orders two drinks.

There's much speculation in the bar about why he's done this and everybody feels a bit sorry for him, thinking one of his brothers must have died.

The barman walks up and passes on their feelings, but the Irishman just smiles and says not to worry.

'Nobody has died,' he says. 'It's just that I've joined AA and don't drink any more.'

*   *   *

A father and his underage son were sitting in the pub one day having a drink and the old man was teaching the young bloke a little bit about drinking etiquette.

'A gentleman never drinks too much,' said his dad, who had had quite a few himself. 'It brings shame on the family and loss of face.'

'How can you tell if you've drunk too much?' asked the young bloke.

'Well,' said the old man. 'You see those two women over there? If you had disgraced yourself with the drink you would see four.'

'But, Father . . . there's only one lady sitting over there,' said the son.

*   *   *

This bloke gets rotten drunk one night at the pub and can't get his keys out of his pocket when he gets home.

Fumbling around, he spills all the coins onto the doorstep before finally getting the key out.

He's too drunk to pick them up and figures he'll get them in the morning, but when the sun comes up he is woken by his wife who yells out, 'Come and look at this, the milkman has left twenty-two cartons of milk here!'

*   *   *

A woman drove me to drink and
I didn't even have the decency to thank her.

WC Fields

THE SCHOONER

THE POT

THE YARD

WHAT BEER GLASS IS THAT?

THE PONY

5¢

THE SEVEN

THE MIDDY.

A bloke walks into a country pub and sees a sign with the letters WYBMADIITY above the bar. Confused and intrigued, he asks the barman what the letters stand for.

Barman replies: 'Will you buy me a drink if I tell you?'

Bloke says: 'Sure, but what do the letters stand for?'

Barman again replies: 'Will you buy me a drink if I tell you?'

Bloke says: 'I said that I would, so what is it?'

Barman replies: 'Will you buy me a drink if I tell you?'

Bloke says: 'Yeah, yeah, just tell me what the letters stand for.'

Barman replies: 'Will you buy me a drink if I tell you?'

Bloke says: 'You're a bloody broken record with bad hearing. What is it?'

Barman replies: 'Will you buy me a drink if I tell you?'

Bloke says: 'I give up.'

And then the barman came clean and explained to the bloke what WYBMADIITY means . . . again.

*   *   *

A shearer walks into a pub and says, 'Give me a f–––ing beer.'

The barmaid says she will not be spoken to like that and refuses to serve him.

'Look, lady, I don't give a flying f––k what you think, just give me a f–––ing beer!'

Again she says that she will not serve him if he uses language like that.

'For f––k's sake, I want a f–––ing beer, right f–––ing now or else!'

The barmaid takes a deep breath and says she is going to show him some manners. She tells him to get behind the bar and she will show him how to order a beer.

They swap places and the woman says, 'Excuse me, kind sir, could I have a beer, please?'

'No, you can go and get f–––d,' says the shearer. 'You wouldn't give me a f–––ing beer, so f––k off!'

*　*　*

Two Victorians had popped up to southern New South Wales for a holiday and found themselves in a shearer's bar staring at this big bloke opposite them.

The barman noticed their fascination and warned them not to look at the man because he hated people staring and had a foul temper.

Still, the southerners could not take their eyes off the guy and sure enough he came stomping over to them, red-faced and furious.

'What the f––k do you think you're looking at?' he demanded.

'Ah, nothing,' said one before adding nervously, 'it's your perfect teeth, I have never seen such perfect teeth.'

'Yeah, well, they are nice, but stop staring or I'll rip your head off,' said the big bloke before going back to his beer.

Unfortunately the two Victorians continued to stare, unable to look at anything else for too long.

The big bloke came stomping over again.

'I told you, now you're going to get it!' he bellowed.

'No, wait,' said the one who had commented on his teeth. 'It's just that you, well, you have great teeth, but your eyes are even better. They are the most amazing eyes.'

'Yeah, they're pretty good,' said the big man coyly.

'Bet you have never worn glasses,' said the Victorian.

'Nah,' said the big bloke.

It was then that the other Victorian, feeling more comfortable with the situation, decided to put his two bob worth in.

'Nah, you would never need glasses with eyes like that, so who cares if there's nothing for them to hang on to.'

* * *

A big, bulky abattoir worker called Bob was renowned for his love of beer and the quantities he could consume.

The bloke was a legend in the small Hunter Valley town where he lived and was said to put away about twenty schooners a day.

One day he took a bit crook and was talked into visiting the local doctor for a check-up.

The doc asked him the usual questions and then got onto his lifestyle.

'Do you smoke?' asked the doc.

'Nah, mate,' said Bob proudly.

'What about the grog?' asked the doc.

'Yeah, mate, might have a few,' said Bob.

'How many?' asked the doc.

'Geez, I dunno,' said Bob.

'Well, how many would you have in a day?' asked the doc.

'Ahhhh . . . it's hard to say,' said Bob.

'A couple of schooners?' asked the doc.

'Well . . .' squirmed Bob.

'Five?' the doc persisted.

'Mmm . . .' the big fella said.

'Bob, if you're drinking more than five schooners a day you're drinking far too much,' the doctor warned.

'For f——k's sake, doc, give a man a break. I'd f———ing well spill more than that!' exclaimed Bob while taking his leave.